PROPHECY

Compiled knowledge for its manifestation

U.K. Tommy

ISBN: 978-978-795-036-4

DEDICATION

To the Holy Spirit. Gentle guide and source of
the love that binds

CONTENTS

INTRODUCTION

Prophecy is real. It is more than an intelligent prediction, gut feeling or informed declaration. It is just as its source, our triune God.

- Are you one of those who do not understand prophecy and wonder if you can trust what you hear?

- Have you experienced prophecy failure and scared to believe one more prophet?

- How can you identify a fake prophet?

- Do you feel like you have been exposed right after a prophecy?

I have met many people, a good number of Christians, who harbour distrust for prophecy. This feeling may have come from their answers to one or more of the four questions above, which I would like to also consider as four categories.

You are reading this book because the matter of prophecy appeals to you. However, one way to be extra sure that this book is for you is if you fall into any of the four categories because it offers the understanding that you need to deal with your peculiar experience.

Knowledge, they say, is power. The information offered to you in the pages of this book will enable you to deal with fake prophecies and prophets who speak presumptuously. It will prepare your mind to be blessed by True Prophecy rather than feel exposed by it and will provide a guide to help you make it come to pass.

As a pastor and teacher, I have observed the four earlier-mentioned categories while teaching about prophecy. I have taught about the Holy Spirit, the source of all True Prophecy. I have also taught about how to deal with the challenge of accuracy and manifestation of prophecy.

If you are wondering why I am so confident that the contents of this book will add value to your search for answers about prophets and prophecy, especially if you are a reader who believes in the power and sovereignty of God. It is because God does nothing without telling us through the prophets among us (Amos 3:7). So, we must understand what such an arrangement entails and how it affects us to benefit from it.

Guided by scriptures, this book provides principles which, if made practical, can bring prophecy, whether spoken or written to pass in your life. I thought to include a few stories and life experiences to provide substance and proof where necessary without deviating from the subject. In addition, this book will leave you with an assurance of the victory that Jesus Christ gives through His word.

1

THE SOURCE OF PROPHECY

"If a prophet speaks in the name of the LORD but the thing does not take place or prove true, it is a word that the LORD has not spoken. The prophet has spoken it presumptuously; do not be frightened by it" (Deuteronomy 18:22 NRSV).

The source of all true prophecy is God. If you have heard God speak through a vessel more than once and carefully surveyed each message, I am sure you must have noticed something different about how they were delivered. Such an observation can give a clue to their source.

The point here is that messages my come directly from God the Father, the Son or by a connection to the Spirit of God. To tell who a message is from, we need to carefully consider its content.

What this means is that right from the start of the message when an introduction is made to let us know who is speaking to us, till the end, we can tell the source of a message.

For instance, if the message is coming from the Father, all words will have power and finality to them, with the pronoun *I* used very often. You can tell from the content of such a message that it is from our sovereign God to whom nothing is impossible. Furthermore, when the message is from the Son, He may speak about His ministry while on earth, His love for the flock, and may use sentences like: *This is what My Father says*. There are also instances when it may seem like the Holy Spirit is speaking. He enables a connection between us in the physical to messages from God and the spiritual.

Every message contains words and actions of the Father. These words, even if revealed by the Son, are meant to work His father's will. There can be no separation of the source of true prophecy from its content which are put together for a reason. Our triune God (Father, Son and Holy Spirit) is that the source of all prophecy.

Reading this book any further shows an interest in having a better understanding of the origin, nature and purpose of prophecy.

Also, every reader can expect to find in the coming pages a pointer to the qualities we need to respond to prophecy appropriately every single time. They are qualities that ensure its manifestation.

Many people talk about positive and negative prophecies. They even work themselves into a frenzy over issues like delays and hindrances to the manifestation of prophecies they receive. However, among the many issues that catch the attention of receivers of prophecy are those of authenticity and manifestation.

With the many deceptions available today, separating what is original from what is fake has become very necessary. Fake prophets and pastors have manipulated many people with weak faiths through prophecy. That is why this book takes the time to guide its readers by providing the information needed to tell a true prophet from a fake one and a true prophecy from a fake one.

As serious as the issue of the authenticity of prophecy is, this book dedicates quite a number of its pages to another pertinent issue as you will come to agree. It is not if prophecies are positive or negative or if there are delays, hindrances or barriers to their manifestations, but how we respond to them. The right attitude is invaluable when dealing with prophecy.

WHY PROPHECY FAILS

The failure of prophecy can be described as a situation in which God's word concerning a person or group does not occur. In such instances, when a word of prophecy is spoken, it lacks the power needed for its manifestation. As Christians, when we read the books of Daniel and Revelations, we may marvel at the power of the Holy Spirit to gain and share with us deep insights of things to come.

Our God is unlimited in knowledge and power and is the beginning and the end of all things. He is also time and sovereign in all things.

Though there are instances of the failure of prophecy, we must realist that these failures or otherwise are much more encouraged by our lack of knowledge about what prophecy is and how to respond to it appropriately. Some people become bothered by the magnitude of prophecy failure that they begin to doubt the legitimacy of the vessel and the message they bring, thereby failing to respond appropriately.

As for God, He can use anything and anybody. Man has a responsibility to respond with an appropriate attitude when God speaks. Therefore, beyond investigating the source of prophecy to be sure of whose voice we hear and to avoid being ministered to in falsehood, we must act appropriately in response, to ensure that the will of God comes to pass.

As for those who speak prophecy, their lives ought to portray them as being more than mere vessels, rogue servants or hirelings. They should live in righteousness, holiness and total obedience to God; this shows that they understand the necessity to be separated and committed to the things of God. They should also be active members of their local Christian groups and maintain good reputations where they live and work.

To the receivers of prophecy, as we carry out the recommendations in this book, we must realise that God has the final say concerning His word and decides every issue concerning when and how what He tells us comes to pass. We must also realise the urgency to act when God speaks and how our actions ought to be appropriate enough to ensure the manifestation of whatever God promises us through prophecy. So far, be assured of five reasons that may lead to the failure of prophecy as follows:

Presumptuous speaking

The origin of the words contained in prophecy is the Holy Spirit and not human will or emotion. The Holy Spirit emboldens and carries the prophet along to express the will of the Father to the church.

Also, the right to speak comes from the source of all true messages, especially when we know that this source has sovereignty. Speaking outside this source nullifies the message, even if it is spoken with the best of intentions. Such comes without the power to manifest as guaranteed by a sovereign God and also leads to failure.

God honours His word and which lines up with His will. So, when a prophet speaks words that do not come from God, it is presumptuous and guaranteed to fail. Now, prophets can also speak or act presumptuously by behaving in two ways. Firstly, they may claim to have had a dream in which the Lord said so and so, which they then proceed to tell what they heard to the church. Secondly, they may present a false act, claiming that it shows the will of God on a matter. Those present may watch such acts without realizing the falsehood in them. What manifests at the end of all of these falsehood is nothing, absolutely nothing, and all because what was said and done were presumption and so did not carry power.

A prophet who speaks presumptuously, speaks mostly out of negative emotions like greed. They usually go further, ahead of the need to extract and use their deception to control weak Christians. You see, from the forgone reasons why a prophet speaks presumptuously, you can tell that such speech bears no profit for the church, instead it can fill us with vain hopes which are bound to get dashed when the prophecy fails. Small wonder why the Lord is against prophets speaking from their hearts instead of His.

Delivering mere predictions

Prophecy is much more than a prediction of the future based on gut feelings or available statistics. It is different from predicting the stock market because we have enough data at our disposal. Indeed, it is more than what our physical senses can tell us. It is the speaking of messages which as earlier stated, comes from the Spirit of God (Holy Spirit) and not human will or emotion.

Many years ago, a young lady introduced her fiancé to her family. After a few questions on this and that and discussion, the lady's family member felt that the planned marriage was not a good idea. This was because from the deductions of a senior member of the family, who predicted doom if they ever got married, it was a total waste of time to proceed with the union. This same family member, who is famed for wisdom, had done a good job of convincing others about his gut feeling and prediction. His reason was that the young man was not smart enough and had no potential to offer any kind of future to their daughter.

But this was not the mind of God. He was wrong. Well as the story goes, they were eventually allowed to marry and the young man became the best thing to ever happen to that family, if you know what I mean.

God's will and purpose

When prophecy does not align with God's will at all times, it is bound to fail. God may also delay or prevent it from manifesting according to His divine design. For instance, there was Micah's postponed prophecy in which he warned the people of Jerusalem. He spoke to corrupt leadership, assuring them that the Assyrian Army would destroy the city and turn it into a heap, a total ruin. This prophesied destruction did not happen because God decided to spare the city and miraculously deliver it from the Assyrians (Isaiah 37:36-37)[1]. This withdrawal of disaster by God was because of the response of the leadership of Jerusalem to this prophecy. They responded in repentance which caused God to show mercy and relent in His earlier planned action.

Genuine repentance

This has a lot to do with our response to prophecy as earlier discussed. When God sends us a message by prophecy because of our sins or wrong decisions, if we repent and retrace our steps back into His will, whatever disaster was in the message will be averted by the power of

God Himself.

Prophet Jonah pronounced judgment on the people of Nineveh because of their sins. Remember how he spent three days in the belly of the fish? He finally declared to the people of Nineveh:

> *"Yet forty days, and Nineveh shall be overthrown!"* (Jonah 3:4).

This prophecy did not come to pass to the displeasure of Jonah. The reason for this was not because He spoke presumptuously or because he was not a true prophet but how the people of Nineveh responded to his message.

God told Moses years ago that He shows mercy to whomever he desires (Romans 9:15). So when the king of the pagan people of Nineveh spoke to his people and proclaimed:

> *"But let every man and beast be covered with sackcloth, and cry mightily to God; yes, let everyone turn from his evil way and from the violence that is in his hands. Who can tell if God will turn and relent, and turn away from His fierce anger, so that we may not perish?"*
> (Jonah 3:8-9).

God saw their genuine repentance and relented from bringing the disaster He said He would bring upon them. Jonah may not have been excited but had to accept the decision of a sovereign and merciful God.

When there are strong reasons

God listens to reason. We can make a righteous case before Him. Some people argue that making a case before God is like trying to change the perfect will of a righteous God to His permissive one. That is not the focus at this point, but to point out that God listens and a strong case can lead to His show of mercy.

For instance, there was a time the Lord sent Prophet Isaiah to a sick king Hezekiah to tell him to put his house in order in readiness for death. The king immediately faced the wall and began to make a case to get God to change His verdict. He reminded God of how he had served Him faithfully and with wholehearted devotion. He also reminded God that he had always done what was considered good by God. While he made his case, God listened and decided against his death and instead healed and gave him an additional fifteen years to live (2 Kings 20:1-7).

Moses also made a case for the children of Israel after they were set free from bitter slavery in Egypt. They sinned terribly against God, and He responded by telling Moses that He would destroy them. Moses presented his case on three fronts. He reminded God that the children of Israel were His people whom He had brought out of the land of Egypt with great power. Moses also reminded Him that He hated being associated with evil and would not want the Egyptians to do so by saying that the God of the Israelites rescued them with an evil intention in mind. Finally, Moses reminded God of the covenant He made with Abraham, Isaac and Jacob (Exodus 32:11-14).

From the cases presented to God by Hezekiah and Moses, we can see how to approach God with records of our faithful service, contents of a covenant made with Him and standing on who we are in Christ and relying on God's righteousness to reconsider a previous decision. Even after Abraham was long gone, God still kept the promises He made to him. We can make these kinds of cases in prayer to God and get Him to change words of destruction.

When love is involved

God is Love. His mercy prevails over judgment. Paul wrote:

"Love never fails. But whether there are prophecies, they will fail; whether there are tongues, they will cease; whether there is knowledge, it will vanish away. For we know in part and we prophesy in part too. But when that which is perfect has come, then that which is in part will be done away with"
(1 Corinthians 13:8-10).

Since love never fails, God never stops loving us or responding to our love. We must continue to love Him and one another and believe also, that He will never stop loving us too. Remember that it is because of this same love that He sent His only begotten Son to die and change the destruction that was to come our way. Therefore, what should fill our hearts is how to respond to His love, one that knows no bounds (1Corinthians 2:9).

You may feel like the greatest sinner in the world but God still loves you. It's the sin in your life that He hates. If the love of God is understood and accepted, it changes everything. We become reconciled and whatever punishment was declared on us through prophecy would be changed. That is the power of love, it has the power to bring about repentance and mercy. This, however, depends a lot on us and how we respond to God's message. Our respond can draw mercy to us instead of judgement.

---

[1] Except where otherwise indicated, all Bible passages can be read from any translation.

2

THE PURPOSE OF PROPHECY

"But the one who prophesies speaks to people for their strengthening, encouraging and comfort" (1Corinthians 14:3 NIV).

The gift of prophecy has made its way to the top of the list of issues raising controversy among many church denominations today. Christians across these denominations seem to feel differently about the subject. I, like many others, believe in prophecy, but I know that a lot more do not.

Some people who do not believe in the gift of prophecy see it as a tool that was only instrumental in the hands of early believers who laid the foundation of the faith and therefore see it as non-essential or even non-existent in today's church.

Another group worries about the phenomenon of false prophets. They wonder if they can be better protected from them by the church as an institution and its leaders. People in this group have experienced firsthand the harm caused by false prophets, heard or read stories, and as a result, decided to avoid the risk of receiving a prophecy.

While the last group are just indifferent about the whole thing, resulting in a lack of interest. The reason is either because they do not know enough about the gift and how it is received or that they do not understand or need it. Many of them argue that all we need already exists in the Word of God, and as a result which encourages the manifestation of such a gift confuses and makes weak Christians vulnerable.

I believe Christians can reduce their vulnerability and keep themselves safe always by understanding the gift of prophecy. I also think such an understanding can provide the ability to identify, manage or avoid falsehood. The point here is that prophecy in the church still exists and is here to stay, and as long as we continue to depend on and allow the Holy Spirit to fill us and use us, we are likely to experience it and the vessels used to deliver it.

There are several ways that God speaks to man. One of them is prophecy. Jesus is the same yesterday, today and forever. Therefore, He is still interested in keeping fellowship with us today as He did with believers in the early church. His desire to communicate with us is an integral part of this fellowship. It has always promoted a need to listen for, recognise and obey His voice (Job 33:14).

The purpose of prophecy is to strengthen, encourage and comfort. When it meets these three goals in the life of its receiver, it can pass as a *true prophecy*. Let those who were previously disappointed be motivated because the Word of God says:

"Let the wise hear and increase in learning,
and the one who understands obtain
guidance" (Proverbs 1:5).

It is the Word of God spoken to the church that guides and eventually provides understanding. A church may be illiterate yet receive the guidance and understanding they require from God to succeed through prophecy. That is so because it is the revealed Word of God that gives us insight into the mind of God and instructs us, all aimed at building obedience to a loving and sovereign God.

PROPHECY IS A GIFT

Prophecy is characterised by miraculous

manifestations, spontaneity and words that can be attributed only to our triune God. At the beginning of every prophetic ministration in church, it is not uncommon to hear the Spirit of God do an introduction of Himself, a historical background of how God created and has interacted with us and finally, the purpose of His descent. An atmosphere of praise and joy is always conducive for the Holy Spirit to descend and release messages from the Lord with power in our gatherings.

When we become born again, we receive the Holy Spirit, who deposits a little of Himself in every one of us that believes. This deposit changes our thinking, behaviour and ability. Many Christian teachers like to refer to this change in character as the development of the fruits of the Holy Spirit. It is proof of our new connection and nourishment through Christ back to God. They also like to consider ability as power released to a believer enabling him to minister to others within and outside the church to the glory of God.

The more we receive and yield to the Word of God through obedience, the more fruits we have and the better their quality. Going back to the gifts of the Holy Spirit, these gifts are deposited in latent form in all believers by the Holy Spirit and activated at His discretion. That means they are not personal to us as believers who carry them.

However, the gifts of the Holy Spirit can be triggered, developed and coveted by every believer1. Also, the Gifts of the Holy Spirit are not for profit but to be made available to all believers. If we want them, we should pray and ask for any or all of them with good reasons (Acts 1:5-8).

The Bible tells us that God has poured His Spirit upon believers in these last days. It enables children of God to manifest nine gifts for the benefit of the church. These gifts, which are nine in number, are grouped as either revelation, power or utterance[2]. This grouping is determined based on the nature of each gift as presented below:

Revelation gifts

1. The word of wisdom

2. The word of knowledge

3. The discerning of spirits

Power gifts

4. The gift of faith

5. The gift of the working of miracles

6. The gift of healing

Utterance gifts

7.   The gift of tongues

8.   The gift of the interpretation of tongues

9. The gift of prophecy

In the group containing utterance gifts is prophecy. It is a gift that can benefit thousands at the same time. It can inspire and provide guidance and solution. It enables believers to utter the deep things of the spirit and ensures that the church, in particular, is guided in line with the will of God.

PROPHECY IS REVELATION

If you are one of many who have ever peered into the sky while wondering what the future holds, you will agree how much you would have welcomed a peek into what is to come. Through prophecy, the hidden parts of our lives and the future are foretold to us by inspired men who can receive messages supernaturally and relay them to our physical ears.

Prophecy is a gift that reveals the mind of God by utterance for the benefit of the church. Other Utterance Gifts are those of speaking in tongues and its interpretation. However, it is not uncommon to see the manifestation of gifts simultaneously. Such combinations are common with Utterance and Revelation Gifts. A prophet can minister in more than one gift if allowed by the Holy Spirit.

Jacob, one of the great patriarchs of the Bible, became old and about to die. So he sent an invitation to all his sons. He instructed them to gather before him because he wanted to tell them what would befall them in the coming days. He ended up speaking to each of them one after the other.

He wanted them to listen to him and act accordingly. This gathering would not just provide insight into the mind of God concerning the twelve sons of this patriarch or a revelation of what was previously covered up, but it was an opportunity for Rueben (the eldest of the twelve, who had an affair with one of the concubines of his father), to repent and make amends (Genesis 49:1)

Guess what, Rueben did not take advantage of the opportunity that stared him in the face that day when his father spoke. He should have begged for forgiveness immediately after his father spoke. Yes! He should have shown repentance and pleaded. That would certainly have prevented the foretold curse concerning his future. As a result, his innocent children suffered for his inaction. They suffered for years for their father's mistakes. It wasn't until five hundred years later, when Moses was about to die, that their situation changed after he prayed for them (Deuteronomy 33:6).

PROPHECY IS THE WORD OF GOD

Prophecy is the testimony of Christ. God speaks to believers through Christ Jesus, also known as The Word. Without Him, there can be no prophecy. The manifestation of the Gift of Prophecy is clear proof that we have Christ in us and have begun to share in His glory (Hebrews 1:2 ESV).

Jesus says that He is the way, the truth and the life. This truth is the same one spoken about in all prophecies through the inspiration of the Holy Spirit. This spirit searches everything, including the mind of God, to be able to guide us appropriately. He releases power for the manifestation of every word of prophecy spoken.

Prophecy tells of Jesus and the messages given to Him by His father, which are relayed to men by prophets. We must test every word of prophecy.

The Bible is the word of God. It is a compilation of several prophecies through which God reveals Himself by constantly speaking to humanity and can be used to test other prophecies.

True-Prophecy must pass the test of being lined up with the word of God. Meaning that whatever does not line up with its content must be discarded as false. That is because God's revelation through the Bible helps us understand His character. He does not act outside this revealed character. Another way to put this is, His past actions and words can help us identify inconsistencies in prophecy today. So if you take your wife for prayers and the prophet says: *The Lord has asked me to take your wife to the river and bathe her.*

Line up such instruction with scripture. Did Jesus bathe anybody's wife for cleansing or healing? The answer is a big *No!* Jesus, certainly could not have instructed anybody to do that either.

PROPHECY EDIFIES

Prophecy builds up the church through encouragement and instruction. At difficult times, it becomes the source of comfort to the church (1 Corinthians 14:3). It also reveals the secrets of the kingdom of heaven and the mysteries behind why Christ came through the Holy Spirit (Ephesians 3:5 ESV).

You may observe that the vessel may speak in tongues before and during the delivery of the message. It is a mystery which may not be interpreted or understood. Nonetheless, it helps in the connection to the spirit realm and submission to the Holy Spirit to be used to bless the church.

Interpreting languages in churches is a pertinent part of ensuring that everyone present benefits from messages from the Holy Spirit and goes back home feeling touched or blessed by what they hear. Therefore, where these messages and sermons are delivered in languages other than the one common to all, it just makes sense to translate them. For instance, if a church consists of more than one tribe and there is a language everyone understands (lingua franca), then messages that are not in the language everyone understands should be translated for the benefit of all.

Such a practice, in addition to ensuring that everyone benefits from the message, promotes unity and a sense of belonging in the church. So, for the messages sent by the Lord to have an impact, they must be presented to all. No one should be left behind due to a language barrier.

Have you started to see how prophecy edifies? It is instructive. The Holy Spirit can search all things from the past into the future, including the mind of God, so able to guide the church (1Corinthians 2:10). That is why when we have important decisions to make or need knowledge, skill or answers concerning our walk with the Lord or any other subject matter, we seek the counsel of God in prayer. The Lord, in response, hears us and instructs us accordingly through His Spirit (Psalm 25:12).

Receiving constant edification through prophecy helps us grow spiritually. The words that we receive guide us into spiritual maturity. Also, the exhortations we receive from messages that come as prophecy persuades and encourages us as a church to be strong, walk in faith and love God and one another. They urge us to do the will of God and become more dedicated and faithful to His service. It also assures us, as the church, of the promises of God.

The Holy Spirit delivers messages of comfort in times of difficulty, sorrow and turmoil. The broken-hearted are comforted, and their wounds get attended to through Messages of Comfort. When the hopeless hear the words in these messages delivered to the church, they become able to rekindle lost hope.

Also, when the church falls into need, one form of difficulty or sorrow, the Holy Spirit brings assurance of relief and deliverance in messages sent through prophecy. In these messages, He reminds us of what our Lord said and did previously. He also assures us of His presence and sovereignty and guarantees our victory, which gives us the strength to keep moving (Psalm 46:1).

PROPHECY GIVES VICTORY

Through the power of the Holy Spirit, a Levite named Jahaziel revealed the mind of God to King Jehoshaphat and all the people who lived in Judah and Jerusalem at the time concerning the threat of battle brought by a very well-equipped and large combined army of men from Ammon, Moab and Mount Seir. He spoke about what to do the next day and how God would take up the fight and give them victory (2 Chronicles 20:10-17).

That same God that used Jahaziel is still at work in the church today and sends messages to His children. He still gives them victory through powerful words sent through prophecy. That should be very profound for us because it was words spoken with similar power by the same God that brought creation into existence in the beginning (Genesis 1:1-26) and was used to declare the finished work of redemption on the cross. God wants us to have victorious lives, and that is why He releases power to strengthen, encourage and comfort us through His word (1 Corinthians 15:57).

The revelations found in prophecy are to provide us with the knowledge and power we need to overcome. God reveals to us - His children, the plans of darkness because He wants to redeem us through the finished work of Christ on the cross.

This lifestyle of victory that He has planned for all His children while on earth is why true prophecy must come with a solution that guarantees we become victorious.

Any prophecy given without actions to be performed obediently for a victory is a mere prediction or presumptuous declaration, something like a gut feeling. Such a prophecy cannot give victory or leave the receiver feeling loved and connected to the Lord. We should find out the source of such a message and examine the vessel that delivers it.

Do not be fooled, sometimes fake prophecies also come with solutions which are also phony, but the difference is that they are usually not accompanied by the power of God. That is why the eighth chapter of this book is dedicated to controversies concerning prophets, to decipher fakeness and tricks.

That is the edge we have over the world, knowing that through prophecy, our God reveals secrets to us (Romans 8:37). No matter the challenge we face, the solution is in the word of God. When we ask God for help while in distress, He sends us His word that contains the power to give us victory. So, be it a stubborn sickness, shameful habit or a limitation, the word of God has the power to save, heal and deliver us (Psalm 107:20).

All these are reasons that allow us boldly say that the end purpose of all true prophecy is to build up, admonish, and encourage the people of God. Whatever does not aim at achieving this is not a true prophecy. So, when we, as God's children, learn to respond appropriately and obediently to prophetic admonition and encouragement, we remain victorious. As you read on, you will discover in the pages ahead what exactly an appropriate response to prophecy is and how it works in our favour.

---

[2] Emily Aig-Imoukhuede, The Holy Spirit and You Course no 200005 © 2004 Emily Aig-Imoukhuede.

3

KINDS OF PROPHECY

"But test everything that is said. Hold fast what is good" (1Thessalonians 5:21 NLT).

Every prophetic message has a subject, purpose and target. God always has a reason for speaking. There is always something He wants to achieve in the life of an individual or community and at a self-determined time. Whenever a prophet is speaking the mind of God while ministering through prophecy, it is always a good idea to hear, examine and document every word. As earlier said, doing this can create a reminder or a reference document that can be useful in the future. For instance, if a prophecy is documented, church leaders can refer to them at a later date to ensure that the instructions given by the Holy Spirit for victory are all obeyed. Documentation also helps check falsehood such that if a prophet spoke presumptuously and it did not come to pass, leaders would have records to guide them to establish that it was a false message.

There are different types of prophecies. We can group them according to their unique characteristics like their subject, purpose and target. Though these groupings are interrelated and work together to edify the church of Christ Jesus, we shall group the different types of prophecies according to their target for easy understanding. We have created two broad groups of prophecy: prophecies about things in heaven and prophecies about things on earth.

PROPHECIES ABOUT THINGS IN HEAVEN

We can never really know what goes on in heaven, can we? What is life really like over there, outside what the Lord and the prophets tell us in the Bible? Do you not wonder? I speak about the Lord and prophets because no one has gone to heaven, lived there and returned to provide an accurate account of life there. We have and will continue to rely on testimonies in the scripture and what the prophets tell us until we get there and see things for ourselves, won't we?

Prophets spoke about heaven even before the Lord told us about the street paved with gold and its many mansions. God still tells us these things through prophecy and as earlier stated, other Revelation Gifts. These stories prepare us and provide information about where we will be on the last day.

The Bible contains records revealing how the great dragon (the devil) fought with the angels of God and got thrown out of heaven to the earth. This dragon, described as an ancient serpent and also called satan, is the deceiver of the whole world. It explains how the devil and his demons came to earth and why they have taken up the duty of destruction (Revelation 12:9).

Revelations such as these inform us of occurrences in heaven and how they affect our existence here on earth. And since God does nothing without first telling His secret plan to the prophets, they, like Micaiah in the time of King Jehoshaphat and his counterpart Ahab, can speak about decisions taken in heaven (1 King 22:2-22).

They can also, as contained in the Bible, go a step further to tell us what will happen in the future. They have prophesied that when the beast spoken about in the Bible gets captured, it, along with those who receive its mark and worship its image, will be thrown alive into the lake of fire that burns with sulphur (Revelation 19:20).

PROPHECY ABOUT THINGS ON EARTH

God is the Alpha and Omega. He knows the beginning and end of all things and can guide His children in the way they should take. It is written in the Bible that the Lord reigns in the affairs of men (Daniel 4:17), and He can provide the guidance we need through His word.

The earth and all that is in it belong to the Lord. No one knows it better or is more qualified to talk about it than Him. Sometimes, He speaks about His plans for the whole world, breaking down His agenda for people, their communities and their nations. So His messages may target individuals, addressing their problems by providing solutions through the words spoken. It can go further to target groups and nations, addressing more complex issues that may affect every member of the group. There are reasons for individual and corporate styles of God reaching out to His children through prophecy, and you will find out what they are in the coming pages.

Corporate prophecy

The Lord can decide to speak to us collectively. Even today, He speaks to Christians just as He spoke to Israel and the early church in the past.

This kind of prophecy passes general warning, guidance and reminders. It ministers to the hearing and benefit of everyone in the group or community.

The Lord sent assurances through a prophet named Haggai. He was to give hope to a whole community. God wanted to encourage them with the hope of His presence and assistance. His message was nothing short of a firm assurance to them that He was with them (Haggai 1:13).

Jesus spoke about an entire city. He talked about the collective attitude of people in Jerusalem and the evil they would do. He prophesied about the city of Jerusalem and the role its people would play in the killing of prophets. It was a warning to both the people of the town and the prophets themselves regarding persecution that was rife in that city (Mathew 23:37).

Personal prophecy

We know the Lord also speaks to us as individuals to provide direction and encourage us. Did you know that He also reminds us of His covenants? Yes, our covenant-keeping God remembers His promises and is always delighted to fulfil them.

In our lives, some matters may be private or sensitive and may not require public counsel. In such cases, the Holy Spirit individually delivers messages. These messages, which carry the needed solution for us as private individuals, may not be necessary for church edification but to increase the faith of only the individual concerned. What makes a difference when we receive a Personal Prophecy is our response. It must be one of humility, submission and quick obedience.

I particularly like Paul's example of a response to prophecy because when prophecies become mere predictions of the future, we must quickly match them with the word of God that conveys God's perfect will. So when a prophet prophesied by a symbolic act, the tying of the hands and feet of Apostle Paul using his belt and saying to those present that what they were seeing was what would happen to the owner of the belt (Acts 21:11), what filled Paul's heart and which was responsible for his response was the burning desire to do the will of God. Moved by this desire, he refused to be deterred or weakened by the message of suffering in the prophecy. Though the prophet did not say that God had changed His mind about what He originally wanted Paul to do, what he demonstrated was what Paul would face in the hands of the Jews, which was capable of making Paul change his mind about going to Jerusalem out of fear.

Like in the case of Paul, such messages have the potential to weaken us. The demonstration of the prophet and emotional outbursts of witnesses to such a prophecy can be discouraging, but in such instances, we must sift through all that to do the will of God. The response of Paul is an instructive one for every Christian. No soldier is ever bothered about the emotions of civilians but is always ready to follow the order of his Commanding Officer (2 Timothy 2:4).

SOURCES OF PROPHECY MESSAGES

God has not stopped moving mightily in our favour; He has not stopped speaking to us. If He discovers a prophet among us, He introduces Himself and sends messages through that prophet in visions and dreams (Numbers 12:6). But alas! We ought to be careful because, for every original, there is a counterfeit. There are fake prophets and messages from God. The devil and his agents also speak to try and mislead people, even Christians. That is why we must learn the voice of our master and be willing and swift to obey it. We should be like sheep who do not reject the guidance of their shepherd. They know and respond to it. That is why Jesus said His sheep hear His voice, He knows them, and they obey Him (John 10:27 ESV).

Animals tend to respond more to the voices of people that they know. Continuous interaction between sheep and a shepherd makes his voice familiar.

Therefore, like sheep, we need to learn the voice of our shepherd. All that was made clear to me when I lived close to some nomadic herders a couple of years ago. I discovered through observation that when the herd returns to camp for the rest of the evening and was made to sit around fires, they would only rise the following morning at the sound of their shepherd. They do not respond to the voice of anyone else.

Learning the voice of our shepherd requires us to study the Bible and regularly interact with the Lord through fellowship. When sheep cannot distinguish the voice of their shepherd, they become confused and vulnerable and can easily be misled- and more in the direction of danger. Remember, just like every sheep is directed by a shepherd using a rod, so are we also by our Lord through His word, which comes to us in different ways. Sometimes the word comes through visions. There are also times that they may come in dreams. The Holy Spirit can also speak the word of God through the mouth of someone or something.

Did you just ask: something? Yes, something At His discretion and in the absence of a human vessel, the Holy Spirit can use anything. In the past, He has spoken through inanimate and animate things, like when He spoke to Moses through a burning bush (Exodus 3:4) and when

He spoke to Balaam through a donkey (Numbers 22:28).

Messages received through visions

God sends messages to us through visions. Prophets can receive these messages that carry God's will and the revelation of mysteries and things to come. For example, John of Patmos, the author of the Book of Revelation, was in a vision on the Lord's Day when the Holy Spirit revealed the contents of the *book of prophecy* to him.

Also, King Nebuchadnezzar once had a dream, and woke up troubled. He wanted this dream told to him and interpreted as well. The king threatened to cut up his magicians and astrologers and turn their houses into rubble if they would not tell him his dream and its interpretation. Daniel came to their rescue after the mystery was revealed to him in a vision at night. He and his three friends (Hananiah, Mishael and Azariah) had prayed fervently for it (Daniel 2:1-19).

Messages received through dreams

The Lord revealed the future of Israel to Joseph in dreams. His brothers hated him for these dreams and the favour he enjoyed from their father. His dreams were more than wishes or audacity to dare to consider exerting dominance over his brothers; they were a revelation of how

God planned to use Joseph to execute his divine plan to preserve Jacob. They were also how God wanted to show the future and survival of the whole tribe of Israel (Genesis 37-47).

Many of us, like Joseph, receive this kind of message from God. In our dreams, the Lord reveals the content of the future of our lives. We should pay attention to our night dreams because they are like binoculars in the spirit realm that show us different things and pray that God would bring what He shows us to pass.

Joseph had known the God of his father, Jacob, and remained faithful and devoted to Him throughout his ordeal in slavery and prison. That made him resist sin and the sinful hope and possibility of elevation and favour offered by the wife of his master, Potipher. There was no way he would have received the training he got in leadership and other skills if he had not been sold into slavery and incarcerated. The point is that Joseph may not have stood any chance of being great from home, which was why God allowed his brothers to have their way. Especially not when he was near the youngest, with ten older, more experienced and envious half-brothers. You see, God reveals through dreams, and man must act appropriately in response.

Furthermore, we can tell a lot about people through their dreams. Your dreams can reveal the state of your finances, marriage and spirituality. It can show if there are victories, limitations or captivities in your life. It can also show what your destiny and the will of God are. Also, after a heated spiritual battle, dreams can show us if there was an impact in the spirit realm.

Being careful to note how we feel after waking up from a dream can indicate if it was a good or bad dream. There is no need to fret. God wanted you to know anyway. The next step you take is what matters, and it should be to pray about such a dream.

If ever we feel weighed down by our night dream, talking to a spiritually mature person like a pastor or Christian friend can also be helpful.

Direct messages from the spirit realm

Sometimes servants of God hear instructions loud and clear right in their ears. The Holy Spirit guides them to the messages He wants them to deliver to the church. There are times when a prophet is taken over by the Holy Spirit and given access to the spirit realm, where record files containing the will and instruction of God concerning the church and His children are stored. The contents of these records are then accessed and relayed to the congregation.

In such instances, while this goes on, other prophets present at such a meeting are expected to be alert in their spirits. They are to monitor the ministering prophet and the message being ministered to the church. That would ensure that presumptuous speaking is spotted. The Holy Spirit, in addition to the messages He sends, always provides solutions to whatever challenge needs addressing.

METHODS OF PROPHESYING

No matter how a prophetic message is received, it burns in the heart of the prophet, who acts as a vessel by declaring whatever is received. There are several ways words of prophecy are delivered. The most important thing is to find a way to get the message delivered without adding or subtracting in the most appropriate, timely and accurate form.

Prophecies can be written, spoken or even acted. One or more of these methods can also be used to get a message across. A prophet must resist the urge to promote visibility but concentrate on doing the will of the Lord. When it is not possible to speak to the congregation at services or act, prophetic messages can be written down and passed to leaders. These days a prophet can even send a real-time message out to the pastor for delivery. There is always a creative way to do this. The bottom line is that prophets should ensure that the messages they receive are delivered as received, and to achieve purpose.

Spoken prophecies

Speaking is easily the most common method of prophesying. The prophet receives a prophetic message, then inspired by the Holy Spirit, delivers it to the congregation. This method is commonly practised in our churches today and is the timeliest way to minister in prophetic messages from the Lord.

A great example of a spoken prophecy in the Bible was by Christ Jesus Himself when He spoke about the destruction of a temple in Jerusalem. While walking away from the temple one day, He began to prophesy and describe the nature of the destruction that would hit the temple. He emphasized that no stone would be left on another afterwards (Mathew 24:1-2).

Written prophecies

I am one of those who believe that prophecies should be preserved by writing them down. When spoken words get written in an unaltered form for all to read, they become future reference materials. Every church is encouraged to track prophetic messages by carefully recording who spoke, when and what was said. It will enable them to ensure that they obey God to the letter when there are instructions.

Evangelist Matthew kept a record of his prophecies by writing them down as inspired by the Holy Spirit, just like John the Beloved. Prophets in many churches, today can also write down their messages. They should not hold back. They can go online or write books, if they must, but they should get the message delivered.

Prophecy by symbolic acts

This kind of prophecy is when the prophet uses objects or does something symbolic of the message to be passed. Bible records show how such acts, which in Acts 21:11, Isaiah 20:3-4 and Ezekiel 4:1-3, were used by prophets like Agabus, Isaiah and Ezekiel to pass messages of God's power and deliverance. And earlier, while trying to explain what personal prophecy was, a reference was made to Prophet Agabus and his prophecy to Apostle Paul using symbolic acts.

Also, contained in one of the chapters listed above (Isaiah 20:3-4) is an example of a prophecy using symbolic acts. God instructed Isaiah to show the people a message symbolic of what would happen. The Lord told him to take off his mourning clothes and sandals and move around stripped for three years as a symbol of the shame He (God), was going to bring on Egypt and the children of Cush. These two nations, which had thought themselves to be greater than they were, had also won public trust at the time. God was ready to shame them and show how helpless they would be when He makes the Supreme Commander sent by the King of Assyria to take them captive and lead them away with their buttocks open and feet bare.

We must not be surprised when prophecies come in spoken, written or symbolic acts. We must also not see symbolic acts by prophets as novel or strange. God can pass a message to us using anything and any method, including symbolic gestures. What is important beyond all this is the source which points to the authenticity of a message and its content which tells us the will and purpose of God and our matching actions in response to it. We shall examine all these in detail.

FAKE PROPHECIES

A prophecy is fake when the Lord has not spoken. It is when the prophets speak their own words sourced from their hearts or when prophets steal the word of the Lord from one another and declare them without being sent (Jeremiah 23:30 ESV).

Time will always tell if a prophecy is true or false. So, one way to test the word of a prophet is to wait and see if it happens. If it does not happen, that indicates that the prophet spoke on his own. Such words would not be in line with the will of God and so would be unaccompanied by His power.

The Lord does not tolerate fake prophets and their lies and has spoken severally about the punishment that awaits them. He sees their hearts and their selfish intentions when they prophesy. Their actions even damage the integrity of fellow prophets and raise false hopes in those who receive these prophecies. When such hopes are lost, the faith of many gets affected.

Their words may seem edifying initially but end up causing more harm than good. Such prophets have destroyed many lives with their lies, which they tell for selfish reasons. They are liars experienced enough to just look at you and cook a message.

In church, they would look at couples who do not have the fruit of the womb yet and exploit them. They would also look at single men and women looking for life partners and deceive them. Their prophecies come with no scriptural backing or solution. To them, it is just a show-one that is for personal benefit.

Fake prophecy leads to apprehension and apathy in the minds of many Christians. How can they tell if it is a message from God? This book answers such questions as you will soon see. In addition, one thing that fake prophecies imply is the existence of an original or what I like to call True Prophecy. The ability to differentiate prophecies that are true from fake ones comes by lining up every word in the message received with scripture and patiently waiting to see if there is a manifestation.

4

THE RELEVANCE OF PROPHECY
IN TODAY'S CHURCH

"Surely the Lord GOD does nothing without
revealing His plan to His servants the prophets."
(Amos 3:7 BSB)

Various controversies trail the exercise of the gift of prophecy. Different views proceed from the lips of many charismatic and non-charismatic Christians that lead to questions here and there that are begging for answers. Chief among these questions found in their minds and which contribute to their mindsets is if prophecies are relevant in the church of today.

God is reliable and trustworthy. He has maintained a character and has not changed over time. His words and promises to man have not changed either- He does not go flaky on His children. He is able to make these promises and ensure a relationship with us by regular communication aimed at building and maintaining closeness, intimacy and fellowship.

Right from the beginning, He kept a relationship with Adam which was why when He came into the garden after Adam and Eve ate the forbidden fruit, they knew Him enough to hide from Him (Genesis 3:8).

God in an effort to maintain this relationship with us even gave up His only begotten son to die on a tree for us and sent the Holy Spirit to edify and guide us. Through this spirit, He has allowed us to have and use special gifts to ensure that we continue to feel connected to Him in various ways. One of which is prophecy.

Prophecy is a miraculous manifestation and revelation of the mind of God in spontaneity through the Holy Spirit which is aimed at strengthening, encouraging and comforting people (1Corinthians 14:3 NIV).

People have limitations and sometimes may become weak and lose their sense of direction. But as we interact with God, because of His compassion, He finds a way to help us through these limitations by messages that come through prophecy.

He pours out His Spirit into people and use them to communicate with others and does this because of the love and compassion He has for us, and to prove it to those with unbelieving hearts. This will not change because God does not change. Just as the Spirit of God and His acts will remain relevant; so will His gifts.

God did not tell us in His word or at any time in the past that He would no longer be communicating to us through prophecy or would not feel like having fellowship with His church anymore (Romans 11:29). I think the problem is us, how we have interpreted freedom and how we are becoming increasingly apathetic towards connecting and hearing from God.

OUR DAYS ARE PROPHETIC

Our days being prophetic means that we live in a time when the Spirit of God has been allowed to fill the hearts of many real children of God. It is a time that was spoken about by prophecy when young people will become filled with the Holy spirit and prophesy.

When we accept Christ Jesus as Lord and seek an in-filling of His spirit, we do not just begin the journey of eternal life but that of a relationship with the Holy Spirit. As evidence of this relationship, we receive supernatural guidance and abilities (discussed in the second chapter of this book). The ability to speak the mind of God through prophecy is one of these abilities.

For those who think that prophecy has or will cease, they are wrong. The Bible does not say that it would cease. Instead, it contains several prophecies about the times we are currently in. A time when the Holy Spirit- who is the spirit behind prophecy, will be poured out on everybody (including men, women and even children). This pouring out of the Holy Spirit will empower many to prophesy (Joel 2:28).

Furthermore, it is always captivating to watch very young people manifest the gift of prophecy. I have even heard about little kids used by the Holy Spirit to speak the mind of God. As long as the church exists and continues to wait for the revelation of Jesus Christ, spiritual gifts will remain (1 Corinthians 1:7).

Jesus, who sits on the right side of His Father, promised us the Holy Spirit through whom He would teach us all things and remind us of His Word (Him). Therefore, if we have indeed received that promise and Christ Jesus still lives and remains the one the Holy Spirit speaks about, there will always be prophecy.

We can go on and on about this but what seems very clear is that God wants to continue to have fellowship with man and has poured a bit of His spirit into every one of His children.

He has been and still is sovereign and wants His will concerning the world and all of us revealed.

GOD STILL WANTS HIS WILL REVEALED

Prophecy reveals the mind of God on any matter. We can be sure that He will not do anything without first telling the prophets. That includes even the secret ones (Amos 3:7). He also reveals secrets to His children (those who please him). This gives his children an advantage over the world and shows that He has sovereign power.

That is why in almost every sphere of our existence, like politics, religion, relationships and others, God still has the final say and prophets declare it. You must be telling yourself that God may control religion but you are not so sure of politics or even relationships. Look, if we take Him out of those critical areas of life, we become vulnerable and may get things wrong and suffer needlessly.

Through prophecy and while King Solomon was still alive, God had already selected his successor. Through a prophet called Ahijah, Jeroboam got to know that he had been chosen to lead ten out of the twelve tribes of Israel. In modern day politics, it is like controlling over 83percent of the votes (1 Kings 11:29-31).

Though Rehoboam, Solomon's son was next in line to the throne, God decided otherwise because He controls politics, even today. David inquired of God whether he should pursue the troop that had raided the city of Ziklag and taken away his family and his men's families. He wanted to know if he would catch them to take back what belonged to them. God responded with the advice that David sought (1 Samuel 30:8 KJV).

Like David, if we enquire from the Lord before taking decisions, including those related to relationship, we would receive the guidance we need. Besides, who is better able to tell us who to marry than the one that knows us all. God provides such answers through prophecy. When Joseph considered ending his relationship with Mary, did God not speak to him in a dream encouraging him to go ahead and marry Mary? (Mathew 1:20).

God still wants to purify the hearts of His children and guide them through His Word and so continues to speak to us by His Son, whom He appointed as the heir of all things and who was there when the world was created. The name of His son is Jesus, who is also the head of the church. He still speaks. His testimony is the spirit of the prophecy of today, and He speaks through prophetic vessels to the church because He lives (Revelations 19:10).

GOD'S POWER BACKS PROPHECY

The word of God carries power. Since the beginning, this powerful word of God has contained the power needed for the work of creation in the beginning and now ministry. It has been powerful enough to sustain what God created. When He speaks, His spirit immediately releases the power for its accomplishment.

Now, since the power of God accompanies His word, when we have problems, God does not need to come to us physically. What He does is send His word. Prophecy can only be backed by the power of God if it contains the word of God and not presumptuous speech. Such a message causes the Holy Ghost to release the power to bring whatever is spoken to pass.

As we dig deeper into prophecy, we shall discover how it relates to the word of God and establish what Real Prophecy should be beyond the knowledge that it carries with it the power for manifestation because it is spoken out of the mind of God and not the emotions of the vessel that speaks. We must be sensitive enough to identify and respond to the will of God when we hear it.

The Holy Spirit, through prophecy, has called many into service of the Lord. You must have heard of people who were called to be ministers by the Holy Spirit. I like the experience of Paul and Barnabas, who were members of the church at Antioch, who were part of several prophets and teachers ministering there. One day during a fast, the Holy Spirit said:

"Set apart for me Barnabas and Saul for the work to which I have called them" (Acts 13:2).

And that was it! The same thing also happens today. I can say this very confidently because like many, I was also called that way and anointed for the work I was to perform.

Prophecy can be written down- just like the times when man was inspired to write the Bible (Revelation 1:1-3). And now, since the word of God can be put into written form, when a minister reads it and receives any insight or instruction from it, then proceeds to present it to the congregation, that minister prophesies. This kind of speaking pleases the Lord and carries His power. It can be observed in many of today's churches (1Peter 4:11).

So, to make a case for the relevance of prophecy in the church today, we must carefully consider the content of every paragraph in this chapter. Hopefully, we will collectively arrive at the answer to the question—an emphatic *yes*.

The relevance of prophecy in the church today goes far beyond providing an insight into the mystery of Christ in us and the mind of God Himself on different matters but enables the obedience of faith and is proof that Jesus lives and loves us.

5

GOD'S GLORY THROUGH THE REVELATION OF SECRETS

"It is the glory of God to conceal things, but the
glory of kings is to search things out"
(Proverbs 25:2 NRSV)

Disciples of Jesus wondered, at the time, why He spoke in parables. So as soon as they had an opportunity, they went to Him and asked why and He responded to their question by telling them that the secrets of the kingdom of heaven have been made known to them but remain hidden from the people of the world (Mathew 13:10-11).

Typically, anyone who does not know the Father or the one He sent would not understand, be interested or determined enough to find out what Jesus meant by His parables. They would be more concerned about the things of this world and trying to meet the approval of men rather than those of the kingdom and the approval of God.

It is the glory of God to conceal things, including things about the kingdom of heaven. He alone decides what is to be hidden or revealed. He also determines when such revelations will come as well as how and where they occur. Through God's divine power, we receive everything that we need for both a godly life and the knowledge of Him who called us to share His glory and goodness (2 Peter1:3).

OUR RESPONSIBILITY TO SEARCH OUT WHAT IS HIDDEN

It should be more than a responsibility to search out things about God, His will and His kingdom we should have this longing and it should resonate deep within our hearts as Christians.

When we get to know the Lord, our response to His love fills us with a desire to reciprocate this love and so for that reason, we develop a burning desire to know Him more and a burden to search out things about Him that we previously did not know.

These things about our sovereign God and His kingdom which were hidden from us when we were in the world, start being revealed.

It is the glory of God to conceal things from us. We share in this glory when we search them out. The more we know God, the more we discover His expectations and our limitations. The more we know Him the more we realise who we are and our purpose here on earth. Only He can reveal our true purpose in this world and here after. Indeed, the more we know Him, the more we want to know Him and the more we become like Him.

Our God has infinite wisdom, He knows it all and does not require our counsel on any matter. His sovereign will must be done in the lives of all men. Therefore it is foolish not to search out this will. Living outside His will is like waking up one morning and taking a walk without a destination. It is the perfect example of living life without a purpose (Ephesians 5:17).

WHAT IS THE WILL OF GOD?

Among the various challenges faced by Christians, one of the most sensitive and life impacting of them is finding the will of God on life's issues. God may hide His will concerning the lives of His children in their best interest but gradually unfolds it as we trustfully and faithfully walk with Him.

Consider the purpose of God concerning the life of Joseph, the son of Jacob. This eleventh son of his father was to be an instrument for the preservation of the lineage of his father. See what his own half-brothers did to him because he even considered being above them and imagine what darkness would have done to stop him from being what God wanted him to be.

It is actually the same thing for us. That is why sometimes the plan and purpose of God for our lives may be hidden for a while to protect us from those whose intentions may be bad and from darkness. We need to learn humility, faithfulness trust, wisdom and become well positioned. What this means is that there is a right time for the manifestation of the will of God, a time when we would have been ready

THE PERFECT WILL OF GOD

The perfect will of God draws His approval guidance and blessing. It is His divine plan concerning something, somewhere or somebody and one that He personally supervises. Divinely, God arranges different issues of our lives like our marriages, careers or even where we live and this arrangement can be considered as His perfect will in those issues.

This can be made clearer by the Bible which tells us that God created us and for a reason (Revelations 4:11 ESV), we are not here on earth by accident but by divine arrangement. So we must find what that reason is as a matter of duty, because it is the perfect will of God, and is sure to receive the approval and backing of God.

The problem we have had with all this is that we have many times ignored or been unsuccessful in finding the perfect will of God and ended up in His permissive will. One day, the Lord told me that people who ask Him for spouses must patiently wait but if they become impatient and bring one to Him, He would give them His blessing. That is His permissive will.

The permissive will of God is what He permits and not what He divinely plans. From what He told me, that He has accepted the spouse we choose for ourselves does not mean that that was His will but something that He permits and His walk with us continues.

The danger of not being in His perfect will is that we may face problems along the way and suffer needless pain that could have been avoided by just sticking to His perfect plan. Some people who are meant to become preachers and save souls in Uganda become diplomats and get sent to India and spend their lives never really being at the head but the tail.

You see, we should strive to be in the perfect will of God in all things and if you keep reading, you will find out how.

Obedience to God must be total and on His terms. When God promised Abraham a son, having that son by his wife Sarah was the perfect will of God and not by his wife's maid Hagar(Genesis 17:15-16).

I have decided to use the example of Abraham purposely. This because at a point, he seemed to have made a mistake accepting the arrangement with Hagar but retraced his steps back to the perfect will of God and He, being faithful and merciful, continued His plan for Abraham. So if you feel like you have missed the perfect will of God, just retrace your steps to Him and He will continue with you from where you went out of the plan.

HOW TO FIND THE PERFECT WILL OF GOD

Now that we know that the perfect will of God attracts His guidance and blessing and that many a times, this divine plan of God is usually ready until an appointed time when we become ready. This time is determined by God but we have a must seek with the assurance of Christ Jesus that we will find (Mathew 7:7).

There are ten strategies for those who desire to find the perfect will of God in their lives. Please use them, they have proven to be effective over and again:

1. Act in wisdom

Wisdom is needed to fulfil destiny. Anybody searching for the divine plan of God must first of all submit to God. That is wisdom and requires humility. It requires that we become ready to listen, learn and be transformed. It is also aimed at helping us build the fear of God because anybody that fears God is wise.

Since the first thing we need is wisdom. For those who feel that they do not have but want her, all that they have to do is ask (James 1:2). Wisdom is invaluable for anyone seeking the will of God, it directs us away from the deception of whatever takes us away from the divine path of God and sets us on the path to fully discover the perfect will of God for us (Ecclesiastes 10:10).

2. Prayer and fasting

A good way to begin the search for the will of God is to get on your knees and pray. This is because the divine arrangement and plan for your life was made by God and it only makes sense to ask Him.

As much as possible, if you feel led by the Spirit to fast while on your search, please feel free to do so. Just ensure that you pray as led by the word of God and that it is passionate, intense, targeted at getting God's attention.

As you pray, please do it with this in mind: prayer is a two way thing. So after praying listen to hear from the Lord. The Holy Spirit is gentle and will not force you against your will. This means that not only must you be careful to receive a response from Him when you pray but also ready to willingly give up your desires and plans.

3. Surrendering your personal desires

There is no need to seek God's perfect plan if we intend to follow our own, is there? To find and live by God's perfect plan for your life, you must be ready to surrender your personal desires to Him and take up His for you.

For example, if we want to choose a wife. God can best direct our choice because He knows the hearts of everyone involved. We can trust Him to be honest with us and hence His plan for us. In this plan, He declared how He intends to prosper and not harm us and that we can be sure of a future in it (Jeremiah 29:11).

4. Studying the Word of God

God honours His word and acts according to it.

So regular study of His word can provide us a guide to His plans for us. It can also help us in making our prayers more effectual by providing the word according to which we are sure that God would act.

Studying the word of God also gives us access to records of the actions of God in the past. There are various stories of how God related with people before us in the Bible and since He does not change, we can study the word of God and receive his approval by allowing its content guide our actions and lead us to God's will.

We are instructed to let the word of God dwell in us richly (Colossians 3:16) and we cannot get filled to a rich proportion by this word if we do not study. God's perfect will can be found through His word hence the importance of allowing an in-filling of our hearts by this word. When this happens, it becomes a light to our feet and a lamp to our path (Psalm 119:105), easing the process of finding out the perfect will of God for us.

5. Having regular Christian fellowship

Meeting with other children of God in fellowship helps us grow in the knowledge and fear of the Lord. We learn from each other, become strengthened in the things of God and benefit from various gifts available for our edification.

I knew a young lady who received marriage proposals from two men and had to decide which one to accept. She was invited to one of our meetings where there was a word of wisdom to her that provided her with the guidance she needed.

6. Avoiding sin

Remember that the ability to seek and find the perfect will and plan of God is an exclusive reserve of God's real children and not that of those with worldly wisdom and understanding. As for these children, though they may seem simple-minded, great secrets are committed to them (Mathew 11:25).

Sin assists the devil hide God's plan. First of all it separates us from God, then it stops Him from hearing our prayers, weakens us and increases our vulnerability to attack. In modern terms I can describe any Christian that toys with sin as being like a Combatant without a bullet proof vest (2 Corinthians 6:7).

If you do not live a life of holiness you cannot fulfil your destiny. So to find the perfect will of God, we must purposefully decide to avoid sin and the illusive propaganda of freedom presented by darkness. This can only happen by the word of God which purifies and transforms our lives (Romans 12:2)

7. Practice forgiveness

I heard a traditional healer speak on radio trying to advertise his treatments for ulcers and blood pressures, while on one of my visits home. His words caught my attention when he spoke about forgiveness.

He talked about how experience had proven that unforgiveness prevents many of his patients from reaching full recovery during treatment. So before taking any of his drugs, he would encourage his patients to first forgive all offences they harbour.

Jesus taught about forgiveness. He encouraged and practiced it even while hanging on the cross. I have come to realise why, which is because unforgiveness can be very destructive. It has three main settings and they are slavery, bitterness and destruction. We cannot find God's perfect will in such circumstances and may even be prevented from doing so by them.

On the other hand, Forgiveness is the will of God for all His children and it qualifies us to receive God's own forgiveness (Luke 11:4). Within us, it does more than set offenders free; it sets the aggrieved free too. So to find the perfect will of God for our lives, we must learn to release ourselves and this can be achieved when we release others by forgiving them.

8. Seek sound Christian counseling

Many everyday life issues can be solved by Christian counseling including how to find the perfect will of God because it focuses on concerns in every part of the life of a Christian. Many churches have trained counselors for this service who combine theology, psychology and scripture to help provide guidance with struggling Christians.

We can also speak with more experienced Christians or pastors who can also guide us appropriately. I have heard people say that a problem shared is one that is half solved. So while trying to find the will of God on any matter in addition to all the other principles mentioned above, Christian counseling can be very helpful.

9. Be calm, learn to wait

Calmness is when you can find some peace, even in the midst of the issues that cause worry. In this case, it is not allowing yourself get into any kind of frenzy while seeking the will of God. Jesus calmed the storm on the lake by saying:

"Peace, be still" (Mark 4:39)

So you must rely on Him to calm your storms too (Mathew 8:23). Avoid running ahead of God; instead, follow His lead. Being calm requires resting your head upon the chest of our

Lord and allowing Him to comfort and guide you as you seek His perfect will for your life. "Why is all that necessary?" you may ask. Because at times, when you have to make very important decisions, you may feel burdened—almost like a woman in labour. That is why Jesus invited people to come to Him and receive rest. He gives peace in such situations to weary hearts

Being calm and learning to wait shows that you appreciate that God is time. He decides when you find what you are looking for. Learning to wait means patience. It is a virtue that is needed, no matter what happens or how things turn out and shows that we have faith that God will show us what His divine plan is concerning our lives (Lamentations 3:25-26). The stronger your faith; the stronger your patience.

10. Constantly check for peace

This principle is very important—you can even call it the *Peace Principle* in these matters. The million-dollar question that needs an answer for this principle to work is: Does your decision give you peace? The Bible says:

"And let the peace of God rule in your hearts" (Colossians 3:15).

That means while trying to find out God's divine plan on an issue, the absence of peace may just be a sign that you have gone off course.

Whenever people tell me their dreams, I usually ask how they felt when they woke up. I try to find out if they felt any despair. While travelling on a bus for business, I had an interesting conversation with lady who had asked me for advice concerning a marriage proposal she had received. It was a tough one because there were a few circumstances of concern. The man concerned did not live in the country, her parents were not happy about the arrangement, He would leave immediately after the wedding and she was not sure of what he did for a living or what she would do after quitting her promising job.

After hearing all this, I asked her how she felt. I wanted to know if she felt peace and guess what? She said no. I considered that as a pointer that marrying that suitor was probably not a good idea and explained it to her. So concerning that decision that you need to make, God is already speaking to you. Check your heart and the circumstances concerning every option available for the one that gives you peace.

WHY DOES GOD CONCEAL?

God is sovereign and may decide to conceal a matter to the glory of His name for a reason and a season without seeking man's opinion.

That means that the nature and duration of such a decision may be unknown. He may choose to reveal what was hidden, in part or in total.

This sort of situation requires diligent leaders who would search out such matters for the benefit of His people. So leaders must be real lovers of God and willing to act on what they discover as part of God's will. Realising the need to do this honours God (Proverbs 25:2) and causes their followers to honour them and even rejoice that they are being led in the right direction and by men of diligence.

For instance, in the Bible, the book of Esther tells the story of one king who decided to search things out. His name was Xerxes. In the story also, there was a man named Mordecai, who attended to the gates of the palace of King Xerxes and was very instrumental in preventing harm from coming to him.

The Lord concealed what Mordecai did from the king until the time was right. When the time came, He laid a thought in the king's mind to review the official records of the empire. While doing so, the king stumbled across the seemingly forgotten records of what Mordecai had done without being rewarded. In summary, that discovery led to the preservation of a whole race previously fingered for extermination by a very powerful enemy connected to the king (Esther 2-8).

OUR SEARCH MUST BE DILIGENT

Prophecy in the church today is God's way of revealing His will and providing guidance to His children. And as earlier stated in previous paragraphs, it is simplistic and even foolish for Christians generally, or as church leadership, in particular, to avoid taking advantage of the gift of prophecy to find out the mind of God on issues (Ephesians 5:17).

When using this gift, we must test the spirit behind it and keep prophets in line by encouraging and motivating them to live holy and righteous lives in the discharge of their ministries.

In the honourable pursuit of the mind of God concerning any matter, if for any reason we run into a brick wall, we must overcome the challenge at the altar of prayer.

God says that if we pray, He will answer us and show us those secret things that seem unsearchable and that we did not previously know (Jeremiah 33:3).

For leaders to honour God, they must search out the gloriously concealed things and be willing to search for the will of God.

They must also lead by revelation. This way, they will be able to rule like God and their actions will show purpose, insight and justice. They will also be able to provide greater motivation to their followers, enough to attract honour and admiration.

OUR SEARCH MUST BE TIMELY

There is a set time for everything. Our search for God must be timely and that is why He calls us to seek Him while He may be found:

"Seek the Lord while He may be found; call on Him while He is near" (Isaiah 55:6).

In addition to the passage above, I also sense a need to be sensitive enough to take hold of an opportunity when it arises. Delaying can lead to missed opportunities for divine guidance, peace, and purpose.

You see, many times it is the god of this age that blinds the minds of those who do not believe that god has a divine plan that must be sought and implemented. This affliction stops them from seeking the perfect will of God (2 Corinthians 4:3-4). Our search must start today because we do not have tomorrow. The truth is that time is of the essence when doing what God wants us to do.

OUR SEARCH MUST BE THOROUGH

Searching for the perfect will of God is serious business. So, our search for it must be extensive and thorough. Now, Let us take our attention to what the Bible says about such a search:

"When my people in their need look for water, when their throats are dry with thirst, then I, the Lord, will answer their prayer; then I, the God of Israel, will never abandon them"
(Isaiah 41:17 GNV).

Thirst in the passage above refers to an earnest desire that only God can satisfy. God has made us know that we can find Him and His will when we look for it with all our hearts. It is a situation where only finding His divine plan can satisfy us. We must be thorough in our search, as if—like they say—our lives depend on it.

WE MUST ACT ON WHAT WE FIND

Action is a key component of the discovery of the perfect will of God concerning our lives. We approach God to find out His perfect will about a matter that concerns us and we do this because we know that the plan was His in the first place, therefore, He occupies the best position to tell us what it is.

Jesus calls Himself the Truth (John 14:6). So we can approach him as the truth and with the assurance of an impartial disposition in all things. Therefore, when we find out the will of God concerning any situation, we have to act by doing exactly what God wants us to do. Our action must be carried out happily, thoroughly, diligently and timely. Our love and trust in God is shown when we act on His word.

6

POWER IN THE RHEMA WORD

"And Simon answering said unto him, Master, we have toiled all the night, and have taken nothing: nevertheless at thy word I will let down the net." (Luke 5:5 KJV)

For us to manifest prophecy, it is pertinent to understand its source. That, in turn, provides us with an idea of the power that it carries. Also, that prophecy should be in line with the Word of God and be non-negotiable.

However, whether a prophecy comes as a message spoken, written or acted by the prophet, we also share the responsibility of ensuring that its inherent power, which brings about the miraculous, is unhindered. Understanding this power and how it works in cooperation with the written and spoken Word of God is of great importance if we must continue to glorify the Lord through powerful manifestations of His will.

THE POWER IN THE WORD

Power is released when we connect to the Word of God and live fully persuaded that it will come to pass. It is a point beyond reading or hearing it but believing it enough to act. The miraculous power of God can be found in His words. It helps draw unbelievers to the kingdom since many of them may not believe unless they see a sign. That is why we must review the Logos and the *Rhema* forms of the Word of God to understand them better and derive as much benefit as possible from them.

Right from the beginning, the Word of God existed. The Word was eventually made alive and even came to live among us with all power given to Him. He was and still is the source of life. God spoke words at the beginning of the world, which caused non-existent things to come into existence. That was how He made the world through His words.

We, being like God, can also achieve the miraculous through the words that come from Him. By Him, we can receive life and make things around us also come alive. Yes, we can! As you read on, you are sure to discover how to do that, to receive all your needs and requests. That is possible because The Word in every situation is like the how. He is the answer.

BREAKING IT DOWN TO LOGOS AND RHEMA

Many parts of the scripture today are said to have been gathered from early Greek and Hebrew renderings. The words *Rhema* and Logos are similar in a sense yet different. They are Greek words that mean The Word of God but are slightly different in that one is more specific than the other. This specificity being referred to here is how one targets us as individuals or communities much more than the other. We shall discover how all that happens as we review the Logos and *Rhema* words.

Over the years, many people have described Logos as the written form of The Word of God. While *Rhema*, on the other hand, has also been described as the spoken form of The Word of God. This chapter will simplify these differences and increase your understanding of how The Word of God is in its Logos and *Rhema* form in the coming paragraphs.

The Logos form of the Word

The Word of God in its Logos form can also be called the Living Word of God. We can call it that because it was zealously preserved by divine assistance for all generations. It is also alive because it is Christ Himself. How can this be? The answer is simple. Logos refers principally to the complete and inspired Word of God spoken by Jesus and written down. Also, since there is no difference between Jesus and His words, as He is also known as The Word (Revelations 12) and since He lives, the Logos word lives too.

The Bible contains several passages where the word Logos was used in sentences to set them apart from others. Comparing various translations would point this out clearly. Some Bible passages in which Logos was used to refer to the Word of God in its early renderings are John 1:1, Luke 8:11, Philippians 2:16, Hebrews 4:12, Mathew 7:24, and Mark 14:72.

The functions of the Logos Word of God

The Word of God has the potential to do a lot in the life of a person. It cleanses, saves, transforms, heals and uplifts, to mention a few. When it is in its Logos form, it serves many functions, one among which is to provide the ability to carry knowledge and convey information about God and His kingdom.

The Bible is arguably the greatest book ever written by men. It contains stories of how God created the world and everything in it. From its contents, we can also read about how He has dealt with men ever since the beginning of the world. Stories of how people in early times encountered and responded to Him provide that perspective. The words in this book not only inform us but also instruct and guide us individually and collectively.

Jesus, through the Logos, tells us who He is, and what He loves and has done. He also lets us know what He expects of us. In all these, Jesus tries to lead us to The Father, who loved us so much that He sent His only Son to die for our sins as proof of this love.

We know God by His Word

We can learn a lot about a person by reading about what the person said or did at different times. Reading up on such information helps us form opinions and understand the character of such a person. As for God Almighty, the scriptures tell us stories of how He has interacted with people from the beginning through what He has said, done and instructed.

If we follow the example of those recorded to have responded to Him in obedience, dedication and wholeheartedness, we will end up victorious like them. The focus in these stories should not be on the people written about in the scriptures but on their God since the objective is to get us to know Him.

Therefore, the Logos form of the Word of God is a compilation of the things Christ Jesus said as captured and preserved in the Bible, which helps us know God and His Christ. It enhances our chances of achieving a life that is rich and eternal. It is the acquisition of knowledge that enables us to begin and sustain a relationship with Him and in which we can learn how to respond to Him in total love and submission.

The Rhema form of the Word of God

Now that we know what the Logos form of the Word of God is, we can begin to delve into other forms of the Word of God. That would include its function and purpose to build faith and give life, understanding, victory and power.

As stated earlier, through the *Rhema* form of the Word of God, which has been discussed earlier and is nothing short of a revelation, we can confidently say that the Holy Spirit gives us direction and knowledge for our current situation. That is possible because the Holy Spirit knows all things, including the mind of men and God, and He, through this Word of God, can direct us in line with the purpose of God Almighty for our lives.

A review of how the *Rhema* Word of God works is necessary to better understand its functions and deepen our understanding of prophecies. Remember, the power that comes from *Rhema* can do the miraculous. It can bring to life what was dead. This power is unquantifiable and limitless.

The functions of the Rhema Word of God

Like the Logos, the *Rhema* Word of God exists to carry out a couple of functions related to one another and aimed at helping us increase our level of understanding and faith. It carries the power to give us victory, convict us of our sins and transform us.

It also conveys the counsel of God Almighty concerning any matter and can lead us to His purpose for our lives. When we receive a *Rhema* word, we come in contact with the truth behind God's word. It produces the power needed to bring about miracles of healing and deliverance.

For instance, in Luke 5:5, Simon, an experienced fisherman, received a *Rhema* word. He had been out all-night-long fishing in a lake but caught nothing and was washing his nets, along with some colleagues, when Jesus approached him.

Jesus instructed Simon to take the boat back into the lake for a catch—this time, deeper. If this had happened in our time, it would be like asking Simon to return to where he had just spent the night in vain and repeat the process—something that would go against common sense, experience, and existing data.

Simon's response could have been: *Go back where? Look, that's a waste of time! How stupid do I look?*

But instead, he responded differently—out of humility, respect, and trust for a total stranger. You see, the words spoken to him were not ordinary, but *Rhema*, which carried enough power to bring about the miraculous. And how did it all end? They caught more fish than they could easily manage and had to call for help from the other fishermen who were close by. That is what *Rhema* can do, even today.

Rhema gives understanding

Many people read the scriptures without understanding the real meaning of what they see. What they read remains incomprehensible until it is explained to them by others. That is one of the things pastors do. *Rhema* comes at that moment when a receiver of the word shouts Ahaa! It is when a reader exclaims loudly for no other reason than the discovery that what was previously read or heard seems to have all come together and started making sense.

The Ethiopian Eunuch is a typical example of this. He didn't understand what he read from the book of Isaiah or what actions to take until Deacon Philip[3] explained it to him. He immediately knew what he had to do and openly declared that he believed by saying to Philip:

"See, here is water, what prevents me from being baptised?" (Acts 8: 37-38).

So, when people show understanding or sudden remembrance of the Word of God spoken for any situation, it is an example of coming in contact with the *Rhema* Word of God.

There are several examples of such in the Bible. For instance, Peter, while explaining his actions to believers in Jerusalem, spoke about how he remembered the word that our Lord had spoken to him and how it influenced his actions (Acts 11:16). That is *Rhema* at work.

Rhema builds faith

Our faith grows when we hear the Word of God preached. *Rhema* is received in such circumstances and produces power when put to work. That is because we can, with help from the Holy Spirit, unravel hidden messages when we speak to others about Christ. These messages are the *Rhema* Word of God, bringing hope to the hopeless, and assurance of God's faithfulness through the knowledge of what He can do. Isn't it significant that in Romans 10:17, the Greek word *Rhema* is translated in modern renderings simply as "word"

The point here is that when the Holy Spirit enables you take what is beneficial to your current situation from the Logos Word of God, what you have taken is nothing but *Rhema*. It is gotten by connecting with words spoken by The Almighty and taking out the one that is particularly meaningful for you and powerful enough to change your situation.

Rhema gives life

When Jesus speaks to us, for His word to richly fill us, we must allow ourselves to remember, speak and meditate on it as inspired. By so doing, what we receive becomes *Rhema*. It is written:

"It is the Spirit who gives life; the flesh profits nothing; the words which I have spoken to you are spirit and are life". (John 6:63)

Interestingly, in the Greek translation of this passage (John 6:63), *words* was initially written as *Rhema*. That means we can infer that Jesus is saying in that Bible passage that the *Rhema* Word of God is what gives life. *Rhema* is not just ordinary talk but words which the Holy Spirit gives power to because of who spoke them.

Rhema produces power

Rhema can be gotten from the Logos Word of God. It can also be measured using Logos. The power in the *Rhema* leads to the conviction of sin, healing, deliverance and transformation. That is why when we go out for evangelism, we speak the word and pray while the Holy Spirit delivers the *Rhema* that brings the conviction, repentance and transformation that we desire in the lives of the people we meet.

The word that Jesus spoke in Luke 22:34 that Peter would deny him three times did not affect him, even after the Lord asked him to pray against temptation (Luke 22:46). But when the *Rhema* came to him in Luke 22:61, it suddenly all came together and began to make sense. He understood and felt the impact of what Jesus had said to him earlier. Peter had experience words spoken in truth and power; they were not mere words but carried power. That was why he wept so bitterly.

Rhema gives victory

Remember that to solve whatever challenge we face, the Lord sends to us His word. As we can now tell, it is when the logos Word of God is converted to *Rhema* that the power to defeat the devil and any difficult situation is released. Until this conversion, the Word of God may not even mean much or make any impact. The word *Rhema* can be found in many other Bible passages apart from those earlier mentioned. They include Luke 3:2 and Acts 11:16.

One direct word from God about our situation changes everything. If that one word comes directly after hearing the Word of God or through a prophet, it has the power to transform.

This statement, I believe, will get clearer than it is as we explore the relationship between prophecy and the *Rhema* word.

About the experience of Simon in Luke 5:5, we can learn that the words spoken by Jesus have awesome power. It can transform any negative situation into a positive one. So, when the master told Simon to try casting his nets again and he obeyed, that was it! What we need to do whenever *Rhema* is involved is to yield.

Rhema specifically targets

It is the *Rhema* Word of God that gives understanding and carries the mind of the Lord. So we must strive for the *Rhema* in every Word of God. The question in our minds should be: what is the Lord saying about our situation? And the answer to this question contains the power to heal, deliver, save and transform our circumstances. This answer is also the will and divine plan of God Almighty.

Many people say that the Word of God has everlasting vitality. That is not unrelated to the fact that each time they come in contact with it, there is a release of *Rhema* for their current situation. They always take something new away after making contact with these powerful words from God Almighty.

SIMILARITIES BETWEEN PROPHECY AND RHEMA WORD

Finding similarities between prophecy and the *Rhema* Word of God will surely help us connect the dots and better understand if there is a relationship between them. Since prophecy is the Word of God, can *Rhema* come through prophecy? Or is prophecy also *Rhema*? The answers to these questions are in whatever conclusion you make after reading this section.

The Holy Spirit is the custodian of the power of God. He is the spirit that enables us to prophesy and also ministers *Rhema* to us from the Word of God, which He does by reminding us of the powerful messages in what Christ Jesus said that were documented in the Bible or perhaps, I should say, as Logos. He also convicts us of our sins, enables transformation and releases the power that should accompany the word. That means that both prophecy and *Rhema* are given by the same spirit.

The *Rhema* Word of God gives us a word for our current situation. It is Christ speaking directly to us. It is similar to a prophecy and tells us the mind of God Almighty concerning any particular circumstance. It usually comes to us as individuals or as a community. The point is that they both carry the mind of God Almighty and give insight into His divine and perfect plan.

The *Rhema* Word of God and prophecy are revelations and are received through the intervention of the Holy Spirit. Jesus is also known as the Word (Revelations 19:13). He is the Word of God described as Logos in the Greek rendering of the Bible and which existed at the beginning (John 1:1), and He is the source of prophecy, the one who edifies the church through prophecy.

There can be no *Rhema* without Logos. Similarly, Jesus is the source and substance of all true prophecy which bears witness about Him. There can be no prophecy without the Word of God. Jesus is in the middle of it all. You see, neither *Rhema* nor prophecy can exist without Him.

Finally, it is instructive to consider the above paragraphs while trying to answer the questions asked at the beginning of the chapter or at least form some opinion of your own on the matter. It is helpful to note that both the *Rhema* Word of God and prophecy can give man the word he needs to deal with whatever situation he faces. They can both impart life (compare John 6:63 with Ezekiel 37:3-14), transform, direct and give insight into the plan and mind of God Almighty.

STEPS TO TRANSFORM LOGOS INTO RHEMA

The Logos Word of God is knowledge, while its *Rhema* form is power. Action is the key that opens the door to the benefits that it offers. You see, the power released through the *Rhema* Word of God makes it more beneficial to us. This power is what produces miracles, solutions and transformations. Remember that whenever we cry out to the Lord concerning a problem, what He does in response to our cry, is send His words. So, we should always look for the *Rhema* word because it carries the solutions we need.

Just like prophecy, *Rhema* is God's message for our current situation; it is His mind and counsel and is powerful enough to bring us victory. Since the *Rhema* form of the word is more beneficial to us, we must always strive to be able to find it. Such an effort requires that we accept the Word of God and submit ourselves to the Lord.

Also, we should realise that the words we receive from God are spirit and filled with life (John 6:63). Therefore, we must desire them, think about them, live by them and allow them to fill us up. The following are guides to transforming the word of God from Logos to *Rhema*:

Accept the Word of God

This whole matter about the Logos and *Rhema* Words of God will never make sense to many people. They are those who wonder how words can make and be made alive and doubt the power we say is released from them. Their inability to understand these things is not surprising, after all, those before us didn't either. And like the Ethiopian Eunuch who had to be ministered to before he could understand the Word of God, so was I.

To accept the word, we must realise that God is trustworthy. We must learn to trust Him and allow Him to guide us by His Spirit to understand what He speaks and the things of the Spirit. Mundane efforts at this always prove inadequate. So, we should first accept Him, then trust Him to give us all the knowledge and strength we need to be His real children (John 1:12).

Submit to God

To Submit to God means to place ourselves under His authority and control in a way that honours Him. It starts with believing that He exists (Hebrews 11:6), followed by learning about Him and the one He sent (Mathew 5:6).

Believing that God exists encourages us to seek to know Him and know Him, which is more than finding out who He is and what He has done, but how He relates with us and what He expects of us. It is a life of righteousness and total submission to His will as part of His perfect plan.

Additionally, in response to God's will, I mean after tasting His goodness and mercy (Psalm 34:8), we need to join in the reconciliation of others to Him (2Corinthians 5:18). It requires being subject to His authority and being ready to do whatever He tells us to do. That is what it means to submit to God.

Exercise spirits

One of the ways to receive the Lord's *Rhema* words is to exercise our spirit when we read the Bible. We should never view the Word of God as mere words but allow our spirits to connect with it from deep down within. That can be accomplished by praying before engaging with the Word of God.

We should ask the Lord to help us make His word profitable by revealing the part that addresses our current desires and situations. Books like, *I am Glory, Breaking through Obscurity*[4] contain experiences intended to guide us on the path to answered prayers. However, only the Spirit of God can do this and also help us connect to the *Rhema* in the Word of God. So, allowing Him to do this can transform our prayer lives in no small measure.

One reason prayers go unanswered is that what we ask for does not follow the will and perfect plan of the Lord. The easiest and perhaps most trusted way, among others, to discover the will of God, is through His word. So, as we pray, we must realise that the effectiveness of our prayer rests on lining its contents up with the Word of God.

Therefore, while exercising the spirit, we ought to pray with the Word of God and listen while trying to connect to the spirit of God. That should be followed by waiting with alertness for the release of *Rhema*. That way, we are not just sure of the answers we seek but are training ourselves and growing our relationship with the Lord through closer interaction with His spirit.

Meditate on the Word of God

This activity involves reading the Word of God and then taking time to think about what we read. Thinking about such words should be done without speaking, in a quiet place and without distraction.

Small portions of the Word of God can be meditated on in our hearts repeatedly. Many Christians practice having *quiet time*—a dedicated moment to speak to God and listen as He speaks back, and often through His Word.

Quiet time for a Christian is an opportunity to meditate on the Word of God and receive

Rhema. The Bible describes a blessed man as one who meditates on God's Word day and night.

Meditation, therefore, should be continuous—like flipping through the pages of a book in search of something. It helps bridge the gap in our obedience to the instruction to pray without ceasing (1 Thessalonians 5:16-19).

Harken to the Word of God

Words like *harken* are quite dated. However, when broken down, they contain elements that deepen our understanding of a particular kind of response. In this case, it describes the most appropriate response of man to the Word of God. The three words that best explain *harken*, and are relevant to us as Christians, are hear, speak, and act. Whenever we receive a *Rhema Word* from God, we must hear, speak, and act on it. That is what harkening is all about

When a preacher speaks during a sermon, we must tune our spirits to hear the deeper part of the message being delivered. This action is necessary as we should now know because it is during such a ministration that the *Rhema* Word of God flows. So, to catch it, we must connect. Also, after receiving it, we should hold on to it and act on it without delay.

Be filled up with the Word of God.

The Word of God is power. Moreso, when it is in its *Rhema* form. It burns like fire in our hearts, one that is also shut up in our bones (Jeremiah 20:9).

In such a state, we become unable to hold it in but begin to act on it. No one can stop the Word of God because it is alive and full of power. When we commit it to memory, we become more likely to receive *Rhema* from it. The Bible advises us to allow the Word of God richly dwell in us (Colossians 3:16). That is because being filled with the Word of God makes us like a brook from which *Rhema* continually flows.

So, if we must strive for this, we must break every barrier to daily contact with the Word of God like sin and the illusion that the world presents to us. We must also realise that the god of this age has blinded the minds of many people to prevent them from seeing the light of the gospel (2 Corinthians 4:4 NIV).

Therefore, let us submit to God and resist the devil so that we can become solution carriers. If we, as Christians, do this, we become relevant to others and pleasing to God.

---

3 One of the seven deacons (Stephen, a man full of faith and of the Holy Spirit, Philip, Prochorus, Nicanor, Timon, Parmenas, and Nicolaus, a proselyte of Antioch) ordained by the disciples of Christ to serve in Jerusalem Acts 6:1-6

4 U.K Tommy, I am glory; breaking through obscurity
© 2021 by U.K. Tommy

7

THE QUALIFICATION FOR A PROPHECY

"All that the Father gives me will come to me, and whoever comes to me I will never cast out." (John 6:37 ESV)

One day, I had a conversation with a church member. It was a discussion that struck a chord by its contents and got me thinking afterwards. On that occasion, we talked about the prophetic ministry in our church and how it was supposed to bless everyone but seemed to fall behind expectations. She told me that from the testimonies of some church members, many of them were not feeling blessed. She then opened up a little more to say that in all her years of attending our church, she had never had her needs ministered to through prophecy.

"Are you serious?" I asked.
She answered, "Yes!"

The thought that nobody had ever walked up to her to talk about God's mind concerning any matter bothered me. I tried to reason what she was trying to tell me or what the implication of it was. She was obviously beginning to feel unloved and isolated, which made her decide to share her experience with me because deep down in her heart, she wanted an encounter with God through His word; she needed solutions.

I came to that conclusion when she claimed that she had witnessed many people receive prophecies and walk out of service guided, comforted and connected, but she had never experienced any of that.

Also, another pertinent thing is that our discussion coincided with when she had challenges with her education and was praying and hoping to hear from the Lord. Her observations led to a question which she kept asking herself in her heart.

Whenever she saw others receive prophecies, she would ask herself the same question. It was a simple question: who is qualified to receive a prophecy?

WHO IS QUALIFIED TO RECEIVE A PROPHECY?

Perhaps like the lady from my church, you also attend a church where individuals are permitted to function in the gift of prophecy but have never been ministered to during any service. That means you must have watched others receive messages without receiving any and wondered why you were not selected. It may have even caused you to question if heaven has a record of your situation or why the gentle saviour keeps passing you by.

The gift of prophecy is for the church. Therefore, it is when the children of God gather in the name of the Lord that it should be permitted. Being Christians makes us candidates who are fully qualified to receive prophecies. More so, with the possession of certain qualities listed below, we can become even more qualified and better positioned.

The description of people who can easily attract the attention of the Holy Spirit and who can cause the release of the counsel of God concerning their situation is below highlighted. If we strive to fit into any or all of them, we can be sure of receiving a prophecy whenever your church gathers. Also, it is pertinent to bear in our mind that it is our responsibility to not just purposefully prepare to open up to the Holy Spirit but to contribute to making the atmosphere conducive for His manifestation.

Making the environment conducive to the Holy Spirit starts with our activities before leaving our houses for a church gathering. For instance, praying and getting into a state of expectation should be done before stepping out of the front doors of our homes. If we do all these, the Holy Spirit will be able to do the will of the Father unhindered. In addition, there is a need to be sanctified and to seek knowledge, understanding, comfort, redemption and hope. Let us look at what it means when we belong to each of the following groups and how that can qualify us for a prophecy.

The sanctified

This term refers to Christians whose lives have been purified. They are those who have allowed God touch their hearts and transform them. Through sanctification, God cleanses them and exchanges their hearts of stone with flesh. He also puts His Spirit in them. The sanctified are separated unto God; they are set apart for Him

Having a heart of stone makes people live without recourse to God. It causes them to sin without shame, even though they occupy exalted positions or claim to know God. Whenever such people allow their lives to become sanctified, they become able to obey

God and avoid sin. They also tend to draw near to God, and He responds by drawing near to them as well, such that when they come into His presence, they attract His attention and encourage the Holy Spirit to act on their issues.

Sanctification must be deliberate and carried out in humility. Those who desire to come before a holy God must first own up to their imperfections, repent of every sin and forsake them (this includes all sinful thoughts, desires, intentions and distractions). After doing all that, they become free from the abomination of their sins and attract the Spirit of God (2 Chronicles 7:14). God assures such people that they will be His and will be successful, protected, and preserved because of their new status as "Sanctified" (Ezekiel 36:22–28).

To become sanctified, the Bible provides us with a clear path. It is through the truth of the Word of God. We can purify our hearts by filling it with God's word and obeying every instruction it contains. It is only the truth it contains that can do this for us (John 17:17)

The prayerful

Prayer is pertinent to every Christian who wants to connect with God. The disciples of Jesus observed how Jesus took time to always connect to His Father through prayer and asked Him to teach them how (Luke 11:1).

And the Holy Spirit, who helped them when they prayed and manifested His gifts, is available to do the same again if you replicate the same effort. It is an assurance of getting a response.

When we, being children of God, pray, God always hears us and answers, especially if He is pleased with us. He also, for that same reason, tells us deep things too. So if we want to be ministered to through prophecy, being in a place of fervent prayer is a good idea because a gathering of spirit-filled Christians engaged in intense prayer is a great atmosphere to get a prophetic ministration. It connects us to God, who is the source of all prophecy. (Jeremiah 33:3).

Through prayer, we can ask God for what we need. Whether we seek provision, knowledge, or guidance, when we ask, the Lord hears and helps us in many ways. The answer to our prayers may be in the form of God teaching us what we need to know (John 14:26) or giving us the power to do things we ought to do (Acts 1:8).

You can begin your journey to prayerfulness by joining the prayer team of your local church, where you can learn from others. When you do this, you will discover that as you pray at such gatherings, you will get connected to the Lord, just make sure while you are at it, your prayers are intense and remember to be humble, determined and expectant.

Seekers of knowledge and understanding

Knowledge in this context goes beyond being skillfully able to take advantage of facts and information that are obtainable through our experiences and education or that of others and to be able to make decisions. Instead, it is the ability to find out what God almighty is currently or intending to do or say concerning any matter.

People who seek to know what God intends to do in any situation have a deep thirst for God's divine plan for their lives. They want to know what His perfect plan is and also want to do His will. Their search leads them to know the Lord more and more and to experience the power of His resurrection. Also their search leads them to revelations that give them insights into the hidden things about the kingdom of God.

God is the one who reveals all mysteries to us as individuals or as a church. Every hidden thing lies exposed before His eyes, so no matter how dark they are, He throws light on them for His glory. So, for us who desire this kind of revelation and who approach and open up to His light, we also share in that glory.

The truth is that God wants His children to seek out the content of His mind at all times, to do His blessed will and live in ways that please

Him. It doesn't stop there because when we seek these hidden things, we also connect with Him and receive more understanding.

Understanding is what we take away from knowing the Lord, and it guides our actions afterwards. I remember when I was a child. Seniors would gather us and tell us interesting stories after which they would ask what the moral of their stories were, and we would say what we learned based on our perception of right and wrong.

That perception becomes sharper by our understanding. The ability to avoid evil comes from that understanding which was received by knowing God.

Jesus thanked God for revealing those things previously hidden from the wise to us who have simple minds. So, there is a benefit when we develop an insatiable thirst for God because we enjoy the satisfaction of His glorious revelation and receive guidance that keeps us away from sin and whatever is evil through the light of His word. The good news in all this is that those that seek will eventually find what they search for.

The seekers of hope

Hope is an expectation. It is a situation when we show confidence in the ability of God to do something. When we build our hope on the love of God, He ensures that we are not disappointed. The Holy Spirit begins to work on our hearts and in our situations (Romans 5:5)

Prophecy is one of the ways we can build our hope. Through it, we have the assurance that God will fulfil His scriptural promises and more. In the Bible, Prophet Ezekiel prophesied that God would again still gather the people of Jerusalem. These words gave hope that God would show His great mercy and power in their lives.

In addition, when we become renewed in Christ, His word can help us find hope that God can help us get our lives back together. He can also ensure that we stay successful. God says He would not abandon us in any way (Deuteronomy 31:6) and reassures us of His promises through prophecy.

The seekers of guidance

Guidance means being led along the path that we should go. It also means that we would never have to be alone. We have the privilege of being led by the one who knows everything and made the plan for our lives - God. He led the children of Israel while they journeyed through the desert and away from slavery.

He sent messages aimed at providing them with guidance in all things and finally became their physical navigation system by going ahead of them as a pillar of cloud during the day and when it got dark, a pillar of fire to give them light. God is always ready to guide us, but we must be willing to fear Him, which means to submit to and obey His instructions (Psalm 25:12).

God still speaks to His people today through the gift of prophecy. He guides them to victory, and just like in times past when He instructed King David on matters of war, He makes His counsel available to Christians to provide victory over every negative situation or foe.

King David even recorded how he had hidden the word of God in his heart which became a guide - steering him in the right direction according to the will of God. He obeyed its instructions and was happy about it. Doing likewise makes God pleased with us and gives us peace. When we are seekers of God's guidance, He sends word to us through prophecy.

The seekers of redemption

Another group that usually receives messages from God is the one that constantly seeks redemption. It consists of people who, whether they realise it or not, need to be saved from destruction. That is so because God is very concerned about getting everyone to repent. He does not want anyone to end up perishing (2 Peter 3:9).

The Lord offers salvation to those who will repent of their sins. That was the reason He sent Jonah to the wicked people of Nineveh because He did not want them to be destroyed (Jonah 3:2). It was also why He led Apostle Paul to write letters to the Romans to shed light on our redemption. He wrote about how it came about through the death of Jesus on the cross (Romans 3:24-25).

So, for those who do not know Him and still live wicked and sinful lives or those who are already part of the church but are still at risk of falling away from the faith, it is in character for God to send messages of encouragement through prophecy to them. That was what He did in the past when He sent prophets with messages that called for repentance and that guided people back to Himself- where safety resides.

The seekers of comfort

Many people, even churchgoers are in distress. That is because they carry heavy burdens and bear unnecessary grief. But the Lord cares about us. He is concerned about how we feel and wants to relieve us of all our distress. That is one of the many responsibilities of the Holy Spirit. He comforts Christians who find themselves in one challenge or the other. The Bible describes Him as "The Comforter" (John 14:16).

To be able to comfort us, the Holy Spirit delivers messages of hope from the Lord to those worn, hurting, and mourning or in difficulty to keep them strong and get them through their problems by His word. Small wonder that in the sermon Jesus gave on the mount, He spoke concerning those who mourn. He described them as a group that will end up happy again by assuring them that they would be comforted (Mathew 5:4).

If ever we feel weak or troubled, through His word, we can find comfort by resting on His chest and allowing Him to comfort us by speaking words capable of soothing our troubles and taking our sorrows away.

THE RIGHT ATMOSPHERE FOR A PROPHECY

God never stops speaking. True prophecy is more than predictions of the future, it is a problem-solving revelation of the mind of God concerning His children. But wait! Are you reading this and thinking you have all the qualifications for a prophecy listed earlier but still haven't received any? Or are you part of a church denomination that does not encourage the gift of prophecy?

The truth is that Christians, one way or the other, enjoy the gift of prophecy if they regularly attend church gatherings where the word of God is shared. You may not have identified it, but it is there. The Holy Spirit makes it possible as long as there is a willing and available vessel. Nevertheless, in addition to preparing ourselves and ensuring that we qualify to receive a prophecy, we can also create an atmosphere for a move of the Holy Spirit. In such instances, the Holy Spirit is able to move unrestricted, and we can identify and decide to yield to this move. A few cases in point of such environments include some of the ones below. They make the manifestation of the power of God smoother.

A gathering of God's children

The gifts of the Holy Spirit are for the church. That means, simply put, that it is best used in the church and for the benefit of its members. Good fathers love to gather their children and interact with them. I grew up in a culture where family members would gather during festive periods. In such gatherings, these members may discuss welfare and other matters. It may also be an opportunity to pass information, make critical decisions and share love in unity.

God is a great father who loves to spend time in fellowship with His children, and just like family gatherings, when He gathers His children on such occasions, He listens and speaks to them to heal, encourage and guide them to ensure that they stay the path of obedience and enjoy the victory that it brings.

Where the Word of God is shared

Have you ever attended a Christian gathering where the preaching was not of the word of God? That would be strange, wouldn't it? That is because the word of God ought to be preached in every Christian gathering. And since the word of God is prophecy which can produce *Rhema* and provides the healing, deliverance and guidance needed by children of God. We have good reasons why we should allow its sharing in our gathering.

Christ Jesus is the word. Sharing Him in our gatherings is evidence that He is the reason for coming together and ensures that people go home with an increased knowledge of and connection to Him afterwards. Doing so makes them feel loved and helps them accept eternal life found in the gospel of our Lord Jesus.

Where there is plenty of joy

The best atmosphere for the release of a prophecy is one where there is a deep emotional connection shared by all who are present. A church auditorium filled with joyful people becomes a conducive atmosphere for the Holy Spirit to move and connect with us. At such times are when He, through vessels, releases words of prophecy to bless the church.

The Lord always inhabits the praises of His people. That means He becomes spiritually part of a meeting in which He is praised. The power in praise cannot be over stated, and the Holy Spirit is attracted to such an environment.

Therefore, if we want to create an environment conducive enough for the release of a prophecy, it should be one filled with praise, and the joy produced is certain to catch the attention of the Spirit of God. It further requires that we make our praise sessions in church more intense when we gather and connect in joy and oneness to the Lord, who will respond by speaking to us.

Where there is a deep connection

God is a spirit. When He made us, He gave us attributes that were both spiritual and physical in nature. Our physical qualities enable us to exist and function as humanly as possible, while our spiritual ones make us godly and also helps us to connect to a spiritual God.

Since our God is a spirit, developing a deep connection with Him would require us to use our spiritual abilities in a diligent search for Him. This search must be with all our hearts without any form of distraction.

So whenever we gather in fellowship, we should respond to the need to pray passionately and deliberately try to bring down the presence of the Holy Spirit through spiritual songs, hymns and acts. We must allow scripture to guide our prayers and allow brethren to speak in tongues to enable them to open up their spirits for a connection to the Spirit of God.

Where there is an available vessel

A vessel is usually receptive enough to be used as a mouthpiece to declare the message of God. Vessels are people chosen by the Holy Spirit. They are instruments to carry out His prophetic purposes. Paul was described as an instrument to carry the name of the Lord to the Gentiles (Acts 9:15) and eventually allowed himself to be used mightily by the Holy Spirit.

Honestly, God can use anything or anyone to deliver His prophetic messages. Many of us have had the privilege of seeing God use children to deliver messages of prophecy to the church. Yes! And if that shocks you, perhaps you should read the story of the encounter of Moses with a voice that came out of a burning bush (Exodus 3:1-10) or the prophet's talking donkey (Numbers 22:21-39).

When the prophet's belly is filled

I found an article that explored the relationship between the Spirit of God and the belly of the one who carries Him. I found it both interesting and educational, as it examined the connection between the "belly" and the "Spirit" It argues that the stomach is a container of many things, and chief among them is the Holy Spirit.

Reading this article was quite educative. It made me remember a story I had heard which once caught my attention. It was a story of a lady with a problem who approached a pastor for counselling and a solution.

The pastor, who had just returned from a spiritual exercise during which he took out days for fasting and intense prayer on a mountain, responded to her numerous complaints by simply giving her a list of what he wanted to eat to break his fast. He insisted on chicken and beans with his rice and a big-sized bottle of cola. When the woman returned and handed over the bag containing his request, he quickly excused himself to relish its content. As soon as he finished eating, he returned to the woman's presence and decreed the end of her challenge.

The lady was livid as she left the church that day. She was unhappy that the pastor did not even calm down to allow her to tell him her story. Well, it turned out that by the time she got home, things took a different twist, and the solution came just as the man of God had declared.

After a nice meal, the Bible tells us how an old prophet had prophesied the mind of God to a young counterpart (1 Kings 13:11-25)

Also, the widow of Zarephath received the miracle of an unexplainable provision in a famine after she agreed to fill the belly of Elijah the prophet, after which he prophesied an abundance (1 Kings 17:7-14). The idea here is that the prophetic vessels of God will always be available and able to carry out their mandates when they are supported and encouraged (Galatians 6:6).

HINDRANCES TO THE RELEASE OF A PROPHECY

Sometimes there are barriers to the flow of the Spirit of Prophecy. They may be physical or spiritual and must be identified and dealt with to enable an unhindered move of the Spirit of God. Therefore, whenever the children of God gather together in fellowship, they must ensure that they are qualified for a prophecy, make the atmosphere conducive for the move of the Holy Spirit and deal with every form of hindrance to the release of prophecies.

Where the leader of a gathering suspects that there are barriers, such a leader must address them in prayer and urgently because such hindrances to the release of prophecy may have spiritual or physical causes. The ability to identify which of these barriers is at work would determine what action to take.

Spiritual barriers

Sometimes, there are barriers in the spiritual realm that may fight against the delivery of messages from the Spirit of God and may occur to prevent the will of God, like the deliverance of an individual or group. One such instance of such a hinderance happened in the days of a prophet called Daniel.

The Bible tells us how the Prince of Persia, a territorial spirit working for the devil, prevented the messenger sent to Daniel by God from delivering a reply to a prayer. From the details of this story, we can tell that an answer was released as soon as Daniel prayed, but there was a delay because the bearer of the reply was intercepted by a demon (Daniel 10:13).
Today, there are still territorial demons going about the business of their master. They work to halt the promises of God in the lives of believers in Jesus by stealing, killing and destroying. Knowing this, places on us a responsibility to receive prophecies prayerfully.

When we gather, and there are signs of the presence of the Spirit of Prophecy, our prayer should be for God to release His power and take charge of the environment such that only words that He sends get spoken. This prayer should be against the works of darkness working against the victory of a congregation and any lying spirit with messages to mislead them. We must speak against all barriers to the flow of God's word.

The Bible advises us to test all spirits. We should try to discern by the Word of God, the spirit behind every prophecy, to ensure that the words are from the Holy Spirit. The Lord usually introduces Himself and refers to scripture to legitimise His identity when He speaks to His church.

It is the responsibility of church leaders at such gatherings to monitor attentively, while ministering through prophecy goes on. The other prophets present ought to remain alert and attentive too.

Sin: It separates us from God. All men are naked before the Lord, and none of their actions is out of His sight. He sees our challenges and knows what we need even before we ask, but our sins prevent Him from acting (Isaiah 59). It is easy for us as individuals to blame our challenges on everything else but our iniquity. But to enjoy many of the benefits of God's love and continue to have unhindered fellowship with Him, we must repent from our sins and embrace righteousness.

When sin is the hindrance to the release of a prophecy, we must respond by praying in one accord to repent and renounce it. Everyone must open up to the Spirit of God in deep contrition and pray for the Lord's forgiveness. We must realise the role sanctification plays in all this and commit to it.

Holding back: It is common for prophets and vessels to fight the desire to be used by the Holy Spirit to deliver messages to the church. Sometimes the reason for this may be that many of them feel that their prophetic messages may not be received by the church and its leaders, especially if it is a warning or carries seeming personal prejudices.

It is not also uncommon to notice rookie prophets who resist the Holy Spirit due to tiredness or stubbornness. Of course, that is why they are perceived as rookies, they lack the experience, understanding, and obedience needed for their calling.

All these may become barriers to receiving prophetic messages in a church. Though holding back comes with consequences for the vessel, it can also place the potential receiver of the message in a harmful state due to the failure of the prophet to deliver a warning or guidance from God.

Prophets need to be encouraged to minister in churches, and where time prevents prophetic ministrations, any message they receive can be written down and passed on to whoever is presiding to avoid failing to deliver them. Occasional training of prophets can help them understand their role and develop the needed boldness to be more effective.

Vessels must also be filled with the word of God and encouraged to meet regularly to pray and sharpen each other. Mentoring can help prophets and vessels develop and become more effective. They can become bold and confident enough to speak to those in leadership and positions of authority by building boldness and confidence.

Elisha was a prophet in Bible times who also led a group known as the "Sons of the Prophet". This initiative, also described as the early school of prophets (2 Kings 6:1-2), provided the training and support needed by its pupils. They were, by staying together, able to gather the skill, support and knowledge needed to execute their ministries.

Physical barriers

Apart from the existence of spiritual barriers, there are also physical barriers which fight against the delivery of the Word of God. These physical barriers are things we can all see, and they prevent prophets from delivering messages from God by constituting some form of distraction. Such distractions may be from friends and those closest to a prophet. They may even be from the environment.

To deal with every form of physical barrier, prophets must focus on doing the will of the Lord only and at all times.

Refusing to give attention to anything outside the message helps this objective. Distraction stands in the way of focus. It takes the mind of a prophet away from the main business of delivering the messages given by the Holy Spirit.

Just as a spirit can set out as a lying spirit (1 Kings 22:22), it can also be a spirit of distraction to stop the delivery of a message and truncate the divine plan of the Lord.

In the Bible, spirits of distraction came upon the sons of the prophets who tried to play the distraction game with Elisha when he pursued the anointing he received from his master. They attempted to get him to consider what was unimportant rather than focus on what was pertinent (2 Kings 2:1-4).

Doing God's work is serious business-one that needs focus and determination. Distractions while doing it can be fatal, just as it was to the young prophet in the Bible (1 Kings 13:11-25). Let us draw an analogy to even pleasurable endeavours such as driving a car (something that many people do every day) requires a lot of attention and focus. It can also be dangerous.

Not being as conscious about avoiding distractions like people or even our phones as required, can lead to injury or fatality. So in my opinion, there is a relationship, one way or the other, between all the causes of accidents on the highways, and they are all linked to losing focus before and while driving cars.

Since leaders, people in authority and the world may be sources of distraction, knowing this can save us from experiencing something similar to the young prophet in the Bible. The old prophet was to the young one, a distraction. A prophet should be a seeker and doer of the Word of God. This word becomes a guide when faced with any form of distraction.

Leaders may try to stop a message from being delivered using their influence or action to cause a loss of focus by the messenger or by using their affluence to create a distraction, but real prophets must resist these things and focus on the business at hand, the one for which they labour.

8

CONTROVERSIES CONCERNING TODAY'S PROPHETS

"For there will be imposters falsely claiming to be God's 'Anointed One,' and false prophets will arise to perform miracle signs to lead astray, if possible, those God has chosen to be His" (Mathew 24:24 TPT)

All prophets are vessels; all vessels are not prophets. That has been the assertion used to explain inconsistencies in the character of those previously considered prophets who fail to meet expected standards. If there were to be an argument as to if there were any truth behind the opening sentence at the top of this page, I bet it would be in favour of those who propose it, won't it? If you are one of those in support, it is probably because you must have met one or more persons who claimed to be prophets but have acted rather shamefully.

Their character must have displayed qualities similar to those found in mere instruments- those who can line up with the likes of Balaam's donkey in Numbers 22:28.

God, in His sovereignty, can use any vessel. Since there is a chance that He may choose to use us, it is our responsibility to make ourselves fit for purpose by being sanctified and ready in every way. When the character of someone who delivers messages from God and carries out His good works does not honour God, such a person is shamefully unworthy of any form of honour.

People who occupy high offices in the church that allow them to minister to others must first build Christian character. That is achieved by submitting themselves to the Spirit of God and purging themselves of sin. Doing so is what teachers of the Word of God described as becoming separated from the world. It makes them vessels that are clean, honourable and worthy of use by the master on all occasions. (2 Timothy 2:20-21).

Many discussions about prophets may seem to put them in the middle of controversies. Right or wrong, people have begun to form opinions and take decisions on how to respond to the issues raised. While you read through the most common ones and determine their accuracy for yourselves, please focus on God's purpose rather than our response and attitudes.

One of the reasons why God established the Prophetic Christian Ministry of the church is because He takes communication with us, His children, seriously. And just like in times long past, God speaks to us through His Spirit, using those of us chosen for this purpose. That God has not and will never change. So, He will continue to communicate with us and still requires, as part of this effort, that we have regular fellowship.

Are prophets and their ministry still as relevant as they used to be in Christianity today? If they are, then they must, like everyone else, operate by the righteous standard of God. Only then will they reclaim the honour that should be theirs and end many existing controversies on the lips of many people who question their character and qualification to deliver messages from God. That will strengthen arguments about their relevance and make them become true blessings to the church of today.

THE CONTROVERSY OF RELEVANCE

As many Evangelicals argue about the current-day prophets, whose role, they say, may not be as necessary for the church today as it used to be, many of their Pentecostal counterparts also believe and claim that all we require for doctrine, correction and guidance is in the Word of God, so they train pastors to minister its contents to the churches (2 Timothy 3:16).

Because of these arguments made by very influential parts of the body of Christ, the conclusion tends to suggest that what they mean is that the role of the prophet is irrelevant and out of fashion in the church today. In trying to provide some form of guide for your thoughts on this, may I ask that we first review previous arguments in earlier chapters about if prophecies refer to the Words of God? If that view is correct, it supports the point that whoever speaks prophecy; speaks the Word of God, which is food for the flock.

Furthermore, unlike man, God is unchangeable. He reveals His intentions to prophets, and just like in the time of Major Prophets like Daniel, He still reveals truths through prophecy, which is out of the control of men. These truths are much more than predictions but are words spoken to establish the perfect will of a sovereign God who directs the affairs of men (Daniel 4:17 KJV).

Also, even today, God calls prophets and anoints them to carry His message to the church. If they had no role to play, He certainly would not go through all that trouble but would long have ended the calls, wouldn't He? God has even, in recent times, spoken to us by His Son, whom He appointed the heir of all things and through whom everything in the world was created (Hebrews 1:1-2). This Son is a prophet of prophets. One who has done much more than carry the Word of God but is the Word of God. And as long as He lives and does the will of His Father by speaking to the church, the relevance of prophets, even today, stands upheld.

Another point here is that the Word of God has retained value and vitality over time. It has always been about Him from the beginning. I drew attention to prophecy being the testimony of Christ in the first two chapters of this book and argued that it was all about Him, so much so that at a point, God sent Him (the Word) to be born as a man and to live with us (John 1:2). Why did God do that? It was because He wanted us to know Him through The Word. And so since He had sent prophets previously, and who all got rejected along with the messages they brought, He decided to send His Word in human form, with the hope that when we see, feel and interact with Him, we might believe.

THE CONTROVERSY OF SELF-INTEREST

The activities of some prophets in recent times have attracted lots of criticism. These activities include a display of self-styled recklessness and strange behaviour, perceived by other

Christians as being out of tune with the discipline and whole-hearted dedication expected of and practised by prophets and as recommended by the Bible.

Some say it is due to poor or lack of formal mentorship today- allowing them to do what they do. The same group argues that while the Holy Spirit teaches everything, mentorship can help groom and provide guidance to upcoming prophets. Also, though some churches already have their mentorship strategies and programmes, there is still a gap because of the absence of a cut-crossing or homogenous guide for mentorship.

Another group believes that beyond the issue of mentorship, prophets themselves yield to worldly desires and have not allowed themselves to be truly sanctified and separated. They have also become self-seeking and pursue personal aggrandisement rather than the will of the Lord Almighty.

Such arguable, recklessness and worldly inclination prevalent among some prophets were spoken in prophecies by their early counterparts- hundreds of years ago. Even now, the Lord still warns them concerning their conduct in His church and the consequences that wait for them.

The warnings from God are all aimed at letting them know that they are in the service of a great and holy God and expected to carry on in a way that shows that they have been called out and separated from those they are to warn. They also show that the Lord knows what is going on in the hearts of men and is constantly providing the information needed to deal with issues. The contents of the various prophecies concerning the character of prophets have been, in a couple of highlights, put together:

- They will speak visions of their minds that will lead to the building up of vain hopes in the hearts of many people. They will also discover the challenges the people face and prophesy messages they have not been given by God (Jeremiah 23:16).

- Many who are not will claim to be prophets, and by doing that, likely to put the children of God in harm's way. They will quickly learn how to speak like prophets and how to profit from doing so (Mathew 7:15).

- Prophets will prophesy lies. They will say what they feel or the messages of others and cook up lies for the people (Ezekiel 13:6).

- They will tell us that they work for God while working for the devil. They will disguise themselves so that we will think that they are doing the work of God but will end up in just as much evil as they lived in (2 Corinthians 11:13-15).

- Prophets will exploit many because of greed. They will pursue money and fame rather than total obedience. Many people will fall victim to this, even in the church (2 Peter 2:3).

- Many people will claim to be prophets and will introduce destructive heresies. They will deny God through their actions and will follow sensuality. They will claim to be prophets and pretend to be spiritual, while behind, they will lead lives led by the flesh. (2 Peter 2:1-3).

Paul was deeply concerned about the challenges the church would face in future. So, while addressing the Ephesian leaders, he said:

"I know that after my departure fierce wolves will come in among you, not sparing the flock" (Acts 20:29).

That there are wolves today in the church should not be shocking, our leaders saw it coming. Instead of dissipating energy in defence or criticism, the effort at this time should be to focus on finding practical ways to protect the flock from the danger that wolves portend.

WAYS TO PROTECT THE FLOCK FROM WOLVES

To deal with the harm that wolves are capable of causing to a farmer's vineyard or to farm animals, it is ill-advised for the farmer to try to work with them or to train and keep them. Simply put, they are not easily trainable or make good guard dogs[5].

Although wolves have been described as non-aggressive by many Wildlife Biologists, they are reputed to be very destructive and dangerous. They have many abilities like, the ability to run marathons and high IQs, which make them more successful and intelligent hunters than many other animals. They also have over 200 million scent cells and can hear up to six miles away[6].

Is it not instructive that Apostle Paul described false prophets and apostles as wolves? You see, wherever there are wolves, they are every farmer's headache. They are destructive and opportunistic, in the best description. We can liken their mode of operation in farms and vineyards to that of the devil in the church, who comes to steal, kill and destroy (John 10:10). Wolves can decide to destroy a whole herd for sport without even eating any.

I remember when my dog Buster, would break into my poultry at night and kill chickens just for fun. I never suspected it because it was calm and helpful while I attended to the chickens. But all that time, my buddy Buster had developed hidden skills in breaking into the poultry and killing hens. I even remember how I had nursed back to health the chicken it had in its mouth the night I caught it. Eventually acquiring the knowledge of who the killer was, I immediately went to work to ensure Buster never had access to another chicken again. That kind of destructive behaviour is what wolves do to sheep.

Just as Apostle Paul used wolves as a metaphor for fake prophets, we will do the same. This metaphor has remained relevant in designing measures necessary to deal with the similar destructive character of suspected-fake prophets. They are measures used by farmers like me, including herders, to protect their flock and are highly recommended in real-life situations in the church to prevent unsuspecting church members from exploitation and destruction.

Apostle Peter's first letter to Christians facing persecution in the Asian Minor contained a bit of advice to be sober and vigilant (1 Peter 5:8). This call to vigilance aimed at keeping the church which represents the flock, monitored all the time. Practical measures, many of which should be proactive, must also be used for this purpose. They include keeping wolves and sheep separated at all times, frequently checking the flock, lighting up the farm and building a fence around the sheep to protect them from wolves.

Always keep wolves away from sheep

Whenever there is a wolf in an area, sheep are vulnerable. A shepherd must never try to make the two co-exist or think that doing so can produce any form of benefit because it is just a waste of time. Rather than doing that, a shepherd must instead find ways of protecting the sheep by denying the wolves access. Some shepherds unintentionally empower wolves when they are allowed access to some part of the farm to help themselves to waste etc. That only increases the vulnerability of the sheep.

Fake prophets have no solution to offer the flock and must never be allowed to operate or mingle freely with them. Some pastors permit the presence of prophets with questionable motives because they believe that they help grow their congregation, but I strongly disbelieve that. Never even give access to ministers you are not sure of. That would be the same as putting your congregation directly in harm's way.

Many prophets, like wolves, move from one church to the other to see which is the weakest to perform their deceit. They can spot weak and vulnerable congregants to tell their destructive lies. Pastors like Shepherds must, on their part, be alert and not allow wolves to operate freely. They should closely observe new members to see what fruit they bear (Mathew 12:33).

Carry out frequent checks of sheep

As a matter of necessity, a serious-minded shepherd who discovers wolves around and does not want them gaining access to the flock must constantly verify the identity and condition of the sheep by checking up on them at every opportunity. Such checks enable the spotting of wolves hiding among the sheep.

The Bible advises that we test all spirits. That also refers to the Spirit of the Prophet. Church Elders must be discerning and able to confront destructive actions. Pastors must also pray regularly for the flock and be willing to check up on them to monitor and guide them spiritually ahead of the destroyer (1 Thessalonians 5:21).

Light up sheep dwelling

The character of a wolf is to lay an ambush in the cover of darkness, but when the resting place of the flock is well-lit, it is made safer. Such dwellings become safer because the sheep can spot intruders and raise timely alarms. The shepherd, on the other hand, can also match sounds of distress or warning with good visibility and so more likely to keep an eye on the sheep and respond effectively to their alarms.

We should also protect the church by filling it with light. That does not refer to physical lighting and fixtures but sound preaching. The point here is that the Word of God is the source of light, and its introduction and maintenance through sound teaching in a church make it impossible for false prophets to access the congregation. They become exposed to the light of the word of God.

Also, strong teaching of the Word of God has the potential to give the needed light that enables the church to detect false prophecies. That is because whatever message is received by the church through prophecy can be authenticated using the Bible. Pastors can better spot wolves and take appropriate action against them to ensure the protection of the flock.

Build a fence around sheep dwelling

An effective strategy to protect sheep is to keep them in a fenced location. It gives the shepherd some peace of mind at night. It's also not uncommon to find fences constructed with material that can conduct electricity. Electric fences keep wolves and other dangerous predators away from the flock at night as long as electricity charges remain in them.

Similarly, for the Lord's flock, righteousness is one of the needed keys. It is a defence that keeps the sheep protected at all times. Through the lives of righteousness that they live, the Lord protects them as His flock by building impenetrable hedges around them.

Christian shepherds have to model Christian character and teach righteousness to the sheep. No dangerous animal can hurt the real children of God. Those among them who live carelessly by playing with sin become vulnerable because their sins expose them to destruction.

THE LIFESTYLE EXPECTED OF A REAL PROPHET

Did you ever know that back in the day, the famous woman called Jezebel in the Bible claimed to be a prophetess? Yes, she did, and we will consider that story further down the line. In the meantime, it is necessary to stress that prophets should understand that their lifestyles can negatively influence how they and their messages are perceived.

One day I heard that some church brethren refused to be ministered to by a certain elder. As soon as I overheard this, I instantly knew it had something to do with his lifestyle. Such a response by church members usually occurs when they have issues with the character of a leader. For prophets, if they live questionably in any way, that can stir up rejection by the congregation. And it also soon causes the church to start rejecting their prophecies.

Prophets must live their lives to the glory of God. Whatever may cause people to cast aspersions on their integrity, the genuineness of their calling or the one who called them must be fought shy at all costs. They should live to obey God at all times. That includes striving to excel in physical things just as much as spiritual ones.

That can only be possible if they fill themselves with the word of God and allow themselves to be examples of obedience in such a way as to encourage the same virtue in others. If they work regular jobs outside their ministries, they should be of good character and meet the Godly standard expected of a Christian like in the past, even those expected of a prophet. The word of God sets these standards.

How can anyone preach or prophesy in the name of Jesus if they do not believe in Him? In many cases, such people do not even try to act as if they do. Prophets have themselves prophesied about the repercussion of failing to live up to the expectations of prophets and the fate of every false, lying or corrupt prophet. In the end, just like their master, satan and beast, they will all be thrown into the lake of fire (Revelations 20:10).

Therefore, every prophet is to yield to these warnings and live right. They should live lives purged of all evil. They must also consistently keep themselves separated from the world. And their lives must show that they are well prepared to do the work they have been called to by God. Anything short of all these would be unacceptable, so their lives should reflect honesty, humility, holiness, purity, love, boldness, freedom from presumptuous speech or the desire for gratification, belief and submitting to Christ.

Honesty

Churches should ensure that all those who call themselves prophets are fit for office. As Christians, we must not tolerate fake prophets like how Jezebel in the Bible was allowed to teach and seduce many to practice sexual immorality as well as eat food prepared in honour of idols (Revelations 2:20).

Many people show up in churches calling themselves prophets today, only to set up an enterprise for financial rewards and lead others astray through teaching messages that confuse and contradict sound Christian doctrine.

Prophets must be teachable and must submit themselves to training before launching out. The food for the flock of Christ is the undiluted word of God, which must fill the heart of every prophet before every debut.

Humility

At one point in time, there was no record of a speaking prophet in Israel for over four hundred years. This period is known as the Intertestamental Period, or what some refer to as the *Silent Years*.

It was a time that had no record of God revealing anything new to His people. Interestingly God never stopped existing during this period and still directed the affairs of His people and ensured the continuation of His divine plan.

You see, God does not need us; we need Him. A prophet should be meek. Real honour comes from honouring God through the quality of our lives and service.

It is ill-advised for a prophet to pursue gain in any form, including recognition. The Spirit of God is not impressed by pride, and when it comes to the issue of honour, even Jesus Himself testified that a prophet would have none in his hometown (John 4:44).

Holiness and purity

It surely will be a waste of time for anybody to do the work of God here on earth and miss heaven, wouldn't it? Without holiness, no prophet will make heaven at last, and while they are here on earth, they are sure to lead many people astray and dampen the faith of many more if they live unrighteous lives. They must be patient, kind, loving and peaceful in all that they do. Their generosity, faithfulness and self-control must never be unquestionable. They must be gentle when dealing with others and joyful while doing the things of God to show themselves as strong and of good character.

Prophets, in addition to sound Christian character, must never be caught involved in sexual immorality or following their fleshly desires. Chances that people will get blessed when ministered to by prophets who live in holiness are higher than by those who live carelessly. Their prophecies are more likely to be accepted. They are the vessels of honour the master spoke about and can use anywhere and anytime because they meet His righteousness standard. They are also sure of spending eternity with Him at last.

Love

Prophets must love God and people too. That is because those who love God obey Him in everything. These prophets should also know He is sovereign, so they should not be afraid to speak His message as instructed. Some people believe that it is not all a prophet sees that he should reveal; I believe that prophets should always ask God for guidance and do as instructed. They should never prophesy in support of evil and must have personal lives that mirror their devotion to the Lord.

Leading the right kind of personal lives requires that prophets carry on with the consciousness that they must become and remain sanctified and separated. To both God and people, they must show love. That requires that they do the will of God at all times and carry out their ministry to the best of their ability and with integrity.

The refusal of a prophet to deliver a message can lead to an avoidable loss, especially if the one who was supposed to receive words of warning fails to get them. So, no matter the gift a prophet has, if that prophet does not have love for God and people, such a prophet would be unable to make needed sacrifices and end up having a much enviable gift, but in reality, having absolutely nothing (1 Corinthians 13:2).

Boldness

The boldness of a prophet should not just be about how messages are delivered, knowing that they come from a sovereign God, but also because of a readiness to expose fake prophets and anyone who may be hiding amid the flock of Christ with the potential or intention to cause them harm. The courage to confront darkness spiritually and physically also constitutes boldness and comes when a prophet is righteous. God wants us to be upright so that we can be as bold as a lion (Proverbs 28:1 NKJV)

When one prophet prophesies, others present at the meeting should pay attention and subject the message to scrutiny. (1 Corinthians 14:29). This is an important responsibility. It enables the other prophets present at such a meeting to ensure that the one speaking does not deviate from the original message sent by God. They must never tolerate a fake prophet or presumptuous speaker.

Free of presumptuous speech

A prophet oversteps bounds by speaking what has not been commanded by God. It is common to see prophets with questionable intentions add to the messages that they receive. Some of them may not have even received any, yet claim that God says so and so. That is not allowed.

When God has not given a prophet a message, but the prophet goes ahead to speak from his heart, that is presumptuous speech. Such speech is offensive to God and challenges his sovereignty. The words spoken in such circumstances are sure to bring God's punishment.

Sometimes prophets speak the messages of others. They relay messages, especially on sensitive issues, which were not originally sent through them. That is not new at all. When Kings Jehoshaphat and Ahab wanted to know the mind of God concerning plans to go to war, prophets spoke each other's messages such that four hundred of them delivered the same message until Micaiah said what the Lord had shown him (1kings 22:1-18). False prophets will burn in the lake of fire, like the devil and the beast.

Free of the desire for gratification

The gifts of God are for the church. That means that they are given to us all. They are received freely and are to be used for the benefit of all, freely too (Mathew 10:8) because whatever God gives is to be used for His glory and not ours. Therefore, the gift of prophecy, like any other received from God, must never be money-oriented.

The mind of God, spoken by prophets, must never be for profit. It is not some commodity or service to be paid for with money or delivered to the highest bidder. If every prophet shows a genuine submission to God by rejecting financial inducement like Peter did when he said:

"Thy money perish with thee" (Acts 8:20 KJV)

It will be proof that they live above the desire for financial gratification. Balaam displayed an even stronger character as a prophet when he was told to curse the children of Jacob by Balak and said:

"Though Balak was to give me his house full of silver and gold, I could not go beyond the command of the LORD my God to do less or more" (Numbers 22:18 KJV).

Believes and submits to Christ

Belief and submission to the Lord is another quality of a prophet, and more so because Jesus mentioned it.

He warned us to ensure that no one deceives us with the claim that they are the Christ and be allowed to lead many astray (Mathew 24:4-5). Many false prophets will come claiming to be the messiah, coming for the second time. They will open big churches, hold the Bible in big crusades, heal sicknesses and speak like genuine servants of Christ. They are servants of the devil, with plans to extract from and deceive the flock.

The attraction to these fake prophets would be the performance of signs and wonders, but Christians must not fall for these lies. We must always test the spirits of these hirelings and profit seekers and allow our actions to be guided only by the word of God.

We cannot submit to a God that we do not believe in. Do we know Jesus? Do we believe that He died for our sins? Have we seen proof of the love of the Father through His actions? There is great power when we submit to God. It means allowing the Lord to live in us and exert

His authority through us.

Prophets who allow the Holy Spirit to have control of their lives receive the power and can use it over the devil. They will speak, and darkness will obey (James 4:7).

THE PASTOR AND PROPHET

There was once a pastor who got posted to a new station. The practice of the church headquarters thought him qualified and experienced enough to take up a new leadership role in one of their regional assemblies. The pastor, taking only his Bible, a Letter of Transfer and light luggage, headed for his new station. When he arrived, he went straight to the church elders and was asked one question, then sent packing.

What was this question, and why was it so important? It was a question they had agreed would determine who becomes their next pastor and which answer would determine their acceptance or rejection of who headquarters sends next. So the pastor was asked the question:

"Are you a prophet, sir?"

With thoughts racing through his mind, the pastor stuttered in his response:
"No, but I am a..."

Before he could finish, the elders stopped him, thanking him for his honesty. All they wanted was a pastor who was also a prophet—a man who would hear from God directly. They were not ready, by any means, to settle for anything less.

They quickly prepared a Letter of Rejection, handed it to the pastor and sent him on his way. When I heard this, it got me thinking deeply. Why would the elders take such a decision? Is the Word of God shared by a pastor and the words of prophecy by a prophet not the same? Does the power in the *Rhema* not come from the Holy Spirit? I was disturbed.

At another time, some church members were discussing the show of bad character by one of the church leaders. Their discussion caught my attention when I heard one of them ask why church authorities even bothered to ordain prophets as pastors, claiming that some church leaders acted out of line because they were more prophets than pastors in their calling. Again I was disturbed because I thought there was no basis or proof that leaders acted out of character because they were prophets by calling, and I also felt that Christian Character was necessary for all.

Someone once said that every real pastor is a prophet. That is because the job of every real pastor is tending to the Lord's flock, which includes feeding them. And what do they get fed with? The Word of God! It also includes multiplying them and protecting them, among others.

A pastor called John Bisagno, in the course of his ministry, compiled a handbook outlining the job of a pastor[7]. He categorised it into four broad areas:

- Being God's man,

- Being a spiritual leader,

- Being an organisational leader

- Being a preacher

In his manual, he described feeding the flock as just one of thirteen responsibilities carried out by a preacher. Therefore, I recommend that any prophet who desires to become a pastor receive the same scrutiny, selection requirements, training and mentorship as his counterparts (1 Timothy 3:1-7). They must all be required to show fruits that point them out as examples of people who have received the Spirit of God (Galatians 5:22-23).

They must also show that they are sanctified and set apart for their desired office. Regarding our gifts, the Holy Spirit gives them to do what He wants us to do. Pastoring requires the performance of several tasks using different gifting. And so if there is one thing we do not want to do, it is make David walk in Saul's armour.

---

[5] https://www.wolfpaws.org › wolf-dogs-as-pets

[6] https://www.visitbigsky.com › articles › post › interesting.

[7] John Bisagno, The Pastor's Handbook
© 2011 (John Bisagno)

9

ACCURACY IN PROPHECY

"But about that day or hour no one knows, not even the angels in heaven, not the son, but only the Father. Be on guard! Be alert! You do not know when that time will come" (Mark 13:32-33 NIV).

One concern that tops the expectation list of those who receive prophecies is the matter of accuracy. In the Bible, Prophet Elisha spoke accurate words of prophecy, and it was at a time of great distress when the city of Samaria was under siege. He foretold a time of abundance with a specific time for its manifestation, in which he accurately stated how much food would cost and when and where it would happen. Even though the stipulated date for what Elisha spoke to occur seemed too close and quite impossible, considering the ongoing situation, it still happened just as he had prophesied because he declared by the leading of the Holy Spirit.

A high-ranking government official who was present when Elisha spoke the prophecy about the city of Samaria considered all the factors that made such a prophecy most unlikely to occur and did not believe it. He even went a step further to express out loud his disbelief and paid dearly (2 Kings 7:1-20).

Many Christians share the concern about the accuracy of prophecy and sometimes spend too much energy worrying about it than how to best respond when they receive such messages. To them, all spoken words of prophecy must be one hundred per cent accurate all the time- which sounds like a reasonable expectation, especially if the job of a prophet is to deliver messages given by God without any additions or subtractions, doesn't it?

The matter of accuracy in prophecy is quite similar to weaving its message, its source, messenger, and receiver into a tapestry of threads to be appreciated as equal in quality, importance and captivation. Concerning spoken prophecy, one aspect alone cannot bring it to its state of perfection. Rather, every part should be accurate, knowing fully well that the source of all messages of prophecy is God Almighty, who is perfect, all-knowing and sovereign.

Outside this source, I worry about the messenger and how authentic the message is in the prophecy delivered. I also worry about the risks related to such a message, being that they come from the spiritual realm to this physical one and may be incomplete, untrue or inconsistent, which may go unnoticed due to how limited we are as humans in character and ability. All of these, in no small way, contribute to making the expectation of many people that messages be one hundred per cent accurate an elusive one.

There are many attributes of accuracy in prophecy. These attributes begin with the ability to relay words heard and expected occurrences, including who will do what, how and where, and ends with when they would occur.

Furthermore, among all the attributes mentioned, the timing of prophecy's fulfillment seems to cause us the most concern. That concern is not surprising because even the disciples of Jesus showed the same interest in when certain events would occur. In their quest for answers, they asked Christ Jesus to tell them when His coming and the end of the age would be (Mathew 24:1-3).

God is Time. He shows His sovereignty and unlimited ability by having the final say on if something would happen or not, and of course, when, as part of His divine plan.

Some Christians say that the more experienced a prophet is, the greater the ability of such a prophet to hear from God, and this includes the ability to state accurate timelines. Therefore, they believe that the higher the accuracy of a prophecy, the stronger the prophet that spoke. In the pages of this book, you will find the guide you need to determine if that assertion is true or false and also find a pointer to how a receiver of prophecy should respond if there is an intention to get to manifest. The idea here is that what makes our responses pertinent is that the right kind is critical to making prophecy happen and is what prevents an eleven-day journey from becoming a forty-year one (Deuteronomy 1:2).

Love was why God sent His only begotten son to die and reconcile man to Himself. It has been the reason for all His dealing with us and His requirement for fellowship, even until now. God's love for us is why He raises prophets to guide and give us hope. So, when the church has a meeting, and people get ministered to through prophecy, God wants them to feel the pouring out of His love. Through this poured-out love, they discern He wants them healed and delivered, and they go back home feeling even more connected and touched by Him.

Now back to accuracy as a universal concern, which involves saying exactly how, who, what and when. In all our concerns about these attributes, and like I stated, *when* ranks highest and gets our attention because it requires patience, faith and trust in God. It has always proven difficult to be accurate about timing, so much so that many feel disappointed when they do not hear precisely from the Spirit about when a prophecy will happen and are unable to plan and maybe even control what and how events unfold.

What do you think would happen if we all knew exactly when the world would end? I bet our repentance would be shallow. It would lack genuineness and sincerity. Suppose we were certain that the world would end at noon next Sunday—can you imagine what would take place on Saturday night and early Sunday morning? Even demons would "clean up" and try to beat the system, just to make it to heaven—some, perhaps, just for fun. Just think about it for a bit. I am very sure many of people would try to deceive God. What do you think?

I have wondered if the fact that prophecy comes in part has anything to do with the challenge of determining exactness at the time of its manifestation. If such a thought has crossed your mind also, then perhaps more knowledge of what time is and how exactly it can relate to a prophecy might provide the answer we collectively seek.

Our sovereign God gives the messages spoken in prophecy and controls every attribute of whatever they contain.

TIME

Time exists from the past through the present and into the future. The whole effort to create and justify a relationship between time and messages of prophecy started one day when the Lord told me something while we were praying. I considered what He said to be very profound-words that have influenced my thinking, teaching and writing. He said: "I am Time".

But how in the world could this be? Remember that our God introduced Himself as "I AM" in the fourteenth verse of the third chapter of Genesis in the King James Bible. He also described Himself as one who does not change. He is, just as He was and would be.

Before this introduction, He gave us an opportunity to record time through the creation of light and darkness, a system that came to be known as day and night. From that time on, we started counting earthly time (Genesis 1:4-5)

God is not affected by our time, He does not wear down, change or lose control (Hebrews 13:8). He knows the end from the beginning and knows what each measure of time would bring because it was all part of what He wanted done. This is so because He existed even before the world was created and long before man understood and began to record time as we now have it (1 Peter 1:20). He, also by His word, brought creation into existence and has sustained it ever since giving order and sequence to what He created through time.

Now, apart from aiding in the ordering of seasons (Acts 1:7 KJV), God's introduction of time has also helped us understand His very nature- that He exists through the past into the present and the future, just like time (Hebrews 13:8), and exerts His will in whatever happens through time as part of His divine plan.

The key idea here is that we should not worry about when revelations will manifest, but rather focus on our relationship with the One from whom all prophecy comes—the One who has the power to create and sustain the words spoken in prophecy.

This is because the one who gives us a snippet into what is to happen, determines the time and the full details of events. It is all about Him. Small wonder He says He is Time.

WHY TIME?

As earlier stated, the issue of time is one aspect of messages of prophecy that has been a source of concern to prophets and recipients of their messages alike. At times, when it seems a bit challenging to provide accurate timing to prophecy, which though not any fault of the prophet, may look suspicious and cast aspersions on the credential of such a prophet.

We must remember that every prophecy is for an appointed time- a time known only to the one who created time and orders everything. So, we must learn to wait patiently and prayerfully for prophecy to happen (Habakkuk 2:3). The point here is that whatever controversy may surround the issue of time in prophecy, it is unnecessary because the Lord Himself is time and determines when His word manifests.

In His power to control, He allows things occur and for His glory, so the most pertinent issue, in my opinion, should not even be time but ascertaining the authenticity of the word spoken by a prophet. Did the words spoken genuinely come from the Lord? If yes, great! Because the Lord, out of love, reveals secrets and shares highlights of things He will allow to happen.

Also, God is neither blind, deaf, nor incapacitated in any way. We must resist the urge to assist Him in bringing His word to pass, lest we fall into temptation or sin. He is sovereign and fully capable of fulfilling His promises without human intervention or assistance. This calls for patient trust as we wait for Him to bring His word to fruition in His own time and way.

GOD HELPS THOSE WHO HELP THEMSELVES

There is a popular saying, often used by non-Christians, whose origins are unclear. Though seemingly designed to promote self-help, it is increasingly used by Christians. The saying goes: "God helps those who help themselves".

Some years ago, someone mentioned that this saying came from the Bible, so I became eager to know the specific verse and embarked on a search but unable to put my finger on it. Who knows, I might find it one day, and it might change my thoughts about its meaning and promotion of the mindset that we can help God, but meanwhile, I advise that we trust God for everything.

Also, after I searched thoroughly for that passage but could not find it, I thought such a statement about God could be misleading since we are to trust the Lord for everything. He is our shepherd, our guide, protector and provider. The desire to resort to self-help has led many Christians into temptation. It does not just show a lack of patience but ignorance of who runs things.

To avoid acting in such ignorance, we should take action as part of preparing for whatever

God promises and trust God for success while avoiding attempts to manipulate the process to succeed.

Another thought on self-help is not to respond in desperation when given a prophecy. This is because such a response can lead a Christian to act rashly or without asking God first through prayer. In rash actions, people tend to ignore the guidance they ought to receive from the Lord and His word and forget that only He has the power to bring what He has spoken to pass. Desperate people try to make prophecies happen by themselves rather than getting filled with hope through prayer, preparation and waiting patiently for God.

The case of Joseph

Speaking through several dreams, the Lord told the young Joseph that his father and brothers would bow down to him (Genesis 37-47). God had plans to use him to preserve his family lineage in Jacob. The revelation of what God wanted to do had started coming to Joseph even while he was still very young. Since I am sure you know this story all too well, let me get to the point here.

To appreciate the story of Joseph more and how the prophecies about him eventually happened, it is instructive to note how he allowed God to make him into what his dreams and plan of God required. This was despite the actions of his brothers, which seemed to be at variance with this requirement.

Notwithstanding, in the end, the challenges faced by Joseph seemed to all be for good. For instance, if his brothers did not get rid of him by selling him to slavery, he would not have learned how to manage men and resources. His leadership training was delivered when he got an opportunity to manage the other staff of Potiphar's house and the men he met in prison.

A combination of what he learned with the fear of the Lord brought him into favour and allowed his leadership skills to get noticed. Some of the qualities of Joseph were:

- A strong devotion to the God of his father, which refers to all Jacob had taught him, even at a young age, to fear the Lord and obey His word.

- ·Joseph never became impatient or desperate, and even when the Butler of Pharaoh, king of Egypt, did not mention him in conversation to the king, he did not become depressed. He did not give up and attempt suicide.

- He also did not become ambitious and wicked when the wife of Potiphar offered herself to him. Greed and lust packed into a bag of ambition, knowing that God promised him some big stuff could have made him consider the sexual advances of his master's wife and try to help himself to the top.

- He allowed God to take him to the palace, and did not bribe or make illegal deals and promises. He did not build up hate and resentment for his brothers or fill his heart with plans of revenge which would have made him sick, resentful or likely to make wrong decisions. Instead of all that, he showed an understanding of what God had done by allowing his brothers succeed in what they did to him.

The point here is that when God speaks, acting to show that we believe involves preparing for what He says and requires seeking a deeper connection to Him.

When God promises us something, to get it, we need to strengthen our relationship with Him by getting committed to becoming and staying sanctified. You see, and as we now know, God has the final say on when, where or how a revealation comes to pass, so we need to rely on Him as we prepare and wait for a manifestation.

The case of Moses

In the days of Moses, many people must have thought that the deliverer would be a man of strength and bravery who would command a greater army than the Egyptians and lead the children of Israel out of slavery, but God had other plans. Moses had to wait in the desert of Midian until he learned to hear from and obey God. Physical strength, political connection or favours from any government official in Egypt were not needed back then by him to achieve the will of God. They are still not, even now.

When God promises us something through prophecy, another reason to trust Him enough to wait is, as they say: "God is always on time"

He is never late. He can decide to take us through a journey of self-discovery, skill acquisition, self-discipline or leadership training (like in the case of Joseph) before handing over what He promised us. God can even give a blessing when we least expect or to be able to save or deliver others. That is just the way He is- sovereign.

The case of Zachariah and Elizabeth

There is always a reason for what time God chooses, so we should accept it. Parents of John the Baptist (Zachariah and Elizabeth) had to wait a bit to have him because of what he was to do for the Lord and when he was to come. So, married couples who experience any delay in having children must understand that it may not always be darkness at work but God. I pray that they believe that their expected children will come at God's chosen time. They should also read and practice the principles that guide the manifestation of prophecy in this book and appreciate that every child has a purpose and a time set to fulfil it.

Knowing exactly when something will happen (time) is exclusively Gods. In addition to understanding this prerogative, it is worthy of note that He determines such things by purpose, and for this reason, we must never take his mercies for granted or be ignorant. Our imperfection and selfishness could cause us to choose wrongly, but we must realise that the Spirit of God is always there to guide us and strengthen us when we need to wait for the manifestation of our heart desires.

DETERMINING TIMELINES FOR THE MANIFESTATION OF PROPHECIES

The awareness that some prophecies are for immediate manifestation while others are to manifest at times in the near or distant future can help deal with impatience and sometimes even despair. With our knowledge that God alone determines when His word comes to pass, when we face challenges, we also should know that He helps us achieve victory by His word, when He chooses.

That means He can speak and decide to bring it to pass speedily or in the future so that we may repent, be better prepared or well positioned. He may also want us to build relationships or keep a covenant. It also helps to pay attention whenever God makes promises to understand what conditions are attached, if any. At times when conditions exist, He makes them clear to us so that we can realise that if we do so and so, we will qualify to receive this and that.

Also, when these conditions are not satisfied, timelines for the manifestation of a prophecy can be affected. All conditions given must be satisfied first before anything happens.

Unconditional manifestations

These kinds of manifestations of prophecy do not place any demand on the receiver and may not even have a particular timeline. God, as part of His divine plan and for the sake of His glory, speaks to us and makes promises which are not dependent on any future action of those specifically involved. His words come to pass without conditions or limits.

Through an angel, the Lord promised to bless Abraham without any condition attached. By the account of Abraham's response when the Lord demanded Isaac, we can tell that there are actions that are capable of provoking unconditional promises and their manifestations and that they are usually sacrificial. When heaven is attracted because God is pleased with us, He may promise us blessings that can be manifested unconditionally (Genesis 22:2 &17-18).

Conditional manifestations

Prophecies that manifest conditionally are dependent on the actions of those involved for their manifestations. They usually come with plain demands that stipulate what we should do and what would follow if we do it. It is because God knows that we can be stubborn and throw care into the wind that He says if you do so, I, in response, will do so.

Joshua was told by The Lord that to become prosperous and successful, he had to meet three conditions (Joshua 1:8). These conditions were:

1. To always speak the word of God

2. To always think deeply of the Word of God

3. To always do the word of God

There are many other examples of conditions attached to the promises of God in the Bible. Let us highlight two of them in the Bible books of Mathew and Roman.

In the Beatitudes, Jesus promises the kingdom of heaven, the earth, comfort, mercy, status and much more but with conditions (Mathew 5:1-11). Also, reading the book of Romans, you will discover that one way to make every enemy a failure is to make God an ally. So, in a contest between us and any person who intends to harm us, we can be sure of victory as long as we have God on our side. We cannot be defeated (Romans 8:31).

Immediate manifestations

There are times when the Lord speaks, and immediately, it happens. You may have seen this happen after a declaration of healing in a service when instantly a change occurs in all those who came for healing. We looked at how Prophet Elisha spoke words that immediately manifested. Though they were words spoken when the city was under siege and stipulated the availability and affordability of foodstuff at a specific time and prices, they immediately came to pass. The reason for this is why I emphasised earlier the importance of the source of a message. In the case of Elisha, because his message was from The Lord, it carried enough power to bring itself to pass, which led to an immediate manifestation. The power contained in Elisha's words was not just strong enough to control the events that followed, but when they occurred too, something only the Lord Himself could have done.

Some prophecies meant to happen immediately may be delayed by some situations, so much so that they may seem like or turn out to be prophecy for manifestation in the distant future. God can even decide against what He says. All these can happen because of our attitudes in response to the message. For instance, due to sinfulness, the destinies of leaders were changed. This happened to Eli the priest (1Samuel 2:30) and also to King Solomon who did not follow the charge of his father, David (1Kings 2:2-4)

Future manifestations

This term refers to prophecies meant to happen at a future date. Perhaps a good example of such a manifestation is that of the end of the world. Nobody knows how far into the future it will be, even the Lord Himself. However, there is a challenge with this, as you might agree, and it is the possibility of a loss of focus while waiting.

Thinking about the third verse of the fourteenth chapter of the book of John can help throw more light on the matter. Jesus promised to prepare a place for us where He was going so that wherever He would be, we may be too. The only way we are sure to experience this is if we stay the course of the way as revealed to us. As long as we remain connected to Him, we can expect a manifestation of what He promised.

Just as there is the threat of losing focus while waiting for the manifestation of a prophecy expected in the future because of weaknesses caused by sin, there is also the opportunity to swing negative ones around through repentance and a commitment to total obedience to God. A case in mind is when God sent a message concerning the future to one of the kings of Judah known as Hezekiah (2 Kings 20:16-19).

The destruction and captivity prophesied against the kingdom could have been prevented from occurring if the four kings that reigned after his great-grandson (King Josiah) had repented and turned from evil. God would have withdrawn His hand against them, which would have prevented the fall of Jerusalem.

THE INCOMPLETE NATURE OF PROPHECIES

Many people have wondered why prophecies never come like a complete story; they wonder why each seems like a selected part of a whole. The details of how a particular phenomenon may occur (when and where) may be missing.

Some people argue that the reason for missing parts in a prophecy is because the prophet may not be *strong* while others say that it is because the prophet decides to deliver just a portion of a message received. The truth is that God does not tell them everything; He never does. He only tells them enough, as maybe required to give us a feeling of connection to Him. This revelation style is because what God wants us to feel when we hear from Him is His love, faithfulness and ability to take us to an expected end.

As earthly parents, we sometimes act like God with our children and may not always see a need or bother to tell them everything. This could be because there isn't enough time to do so, to protect them, or because they wouldn't understand it at all. So, what our children end up hearing is determined by us, they are the information we consider relevant and necessary, and that is after we must have sifted through everything. So when your 7-year-old child says:

"Daddy, when I grow up, I want to be rich"

You respond by saying:

"Sure!"

But the child still comes back to ask how to be rich. You have got to be smart. In such a situation, you certainly won't start telling the child all you have learned and now know about the stock market and all that, will you? No way! You might just say: "You are already doing what you need to. You keep doing your best in school and keep those grades high, and you'll end up rich".

This response is what the child can understand, the rest you will unpack gradually as appropriate in the future.

Since God tells us only as much as we need to hear and act on to experience victory. It means that the prophets are *strong* and thorough in their delivery, may not always get the complete message and can only speak what they receive. Remember that the most important thing in all this is that what we hear from the prophets is enough to give us victory and keep us connected (1 Corinthians 13:8-10). If ever we need to know more, all we have to do is ask the Lord.

Nevertheless, it seems unreasonable to want more prophecies while yet to obey the instruction given in the last one. A survey of how God spoke to Father Abraham in the book of Genesis (Chapters 12-15) shows an interesting trend. You will notice that it was after Abraham had carried out the first instruction that he received a second one. So to know more about what is in the mind of God, we have to please Him. God has not changed.

Another side to the matter is how searching for more and more prophecies can lead us away from what is pertinent. We may even become preoccupied with running after these prophecies rather than the giver. Such a pursuit comes with a caveat, *be careful not to fall into temptation.*

This is because, as we have discovered, there are False Prophets and prophecies. For now, we have the Bible, which is full of prophecies and which we should focus on. Let us also bear in mind that when we have carried out all the instructions contained in what was revealed, we become qualified to receive more revelation. Remember that we listen because God speaks; we have victory because we obey.

10

THE MANIFESTATION PROCESS

"Not one word of all the good promises that the Lord had made to the house of Israel had failed, all came to pass" (Joshua 21:45 ESV)

God is trustworthy whenever He speaks to us, His statements are rich in promises that He never fails to fulfil in our lives. We, as human beings, on the other hand, can be flaky when it comes to keeping our word because of limitations that we may be unable to deal with in character and ability that affect our ability to be faithful.

Sometimes, in our response to God when He speaks, we tend to act in ways that knowingly or unknowingly work against what God says or what we now know as His perfect plan for us.

Such a counteraction usually happens when we permit the erection of barriers through sin, impatience, fear and doubt which can prevent the manifestation of any promise made by God to us through the Word of God.

Concerning the nature of the barrier that sin poses, the Bible tells us that it stands between us and God, who alone has the power to bring His promises to pass. What that means is it separates us from God, such that we lose our right to approach Him, which causes our prayers to go unanswered (Isaiah 59:1-2). When that happens, we may not respond appropriately and end up with even more barriers. We may become impatient and lose hope that God will do what He promised- a situation that leads us to lose confidence in the word of God and develop fear.

What follows is that all of that may lead to a vulnerability in which people find themselves weak and open to foolish counsel and influences capable of causing them to run from pillar to post. A good number of Christians, disappointingly, have also found themselves in the wrong places where they have had to submit to darkness just because they did not know God or trust Him enough to wait for the manifestation of whatever He promised.

Knowing God makes us strong, innovative and bold enough to do things we never thought we could despite whatever challenges may exist around us. On the other hand, not knowing Him can leave us vulnerable or cause us to fall prey to the wolves among us, whose misguided advice we may hear and eventually act on. They might say, "Go ahead if you feel like it. Besides, no one is perfect."

Lies like the one above are what the wolves keep telling the sheep to lead them astray. But if their hearts remain fixed on the hope of what the Lord can do, they will overcome every misdirection of false prophets and wait for the Lord to fulfil His promises.

Patience is invaluable in the manifestation process of every promise of God. It is the ability to calmly wait for God to do whatever He said He would do. If there are times when it seems like time is running out, what we should do is remember this simple truth: God is never late; He is always on time.

Also, some people may find waiting quite hard, even though it is the right thing. They may also view prophecy as something that does not work and may even prefer to take a chance on life-living without having to bother themselves with it but living according to their understanding of what is best (Proverbs 3:5-6).

Regarding the manifestation of the promises of God, the Bible tells us that none of the promises God made to the house of Israel failed; every single one of them came to pass

(Joshua 21:45). Such a report should cause us to wonder- enough to ask the question, how so? Well, your guess is as good as mine: Israel must have responded in ways that must have made it easy for the promises of God made to them to come to pass. If carefully reviewed, these responses can help us put together a guide that informs appropriate responses to promises made to us by God and ensure that we get the same result that the children of Israel got. As documented in the Bible, their responses included:

- Carefully documenting every word that God spoke to them.

- Ensuring that every word that God spoke to them was taught and obeyed.

- Passing down this culture of obedience from father to son and one generation to the next.

- Praying with the word of God to constantly remind the Lord of His promises every time they communicated with Him

Every effort and time used to review what must have constituted the response of the house of Israel to the promises made to them by God are resources well spent. So, after reading this chapter, take a minute to formulate your personal response strategy to the promises of God to you. It will be well worth it.

WAYS TO MAKE PROPHECY HAPPEN

So far, our view is that God does what He says at His own good time and that though there are situations when forces of darkness or people may stand against the manifestation of God's perfect will, it is imperative to develop the right attitude to stay connected to the Lord while waiting. So, before you even ask the question I am sure must be in your heart, let me give you the answer: yes, forces of darkness can use people as agents to stop the promises of God to His children.

King David expressed dismay over people who, without cause, worked against him (Psalm 35:7). It is a reality in life that people you may or may not know can seek your downfall or destruction without known or justifiable reason, but having the right attitude mentioned earlier can, in addition to other basic Christian ones, ensure that the will of God still happens unhindered.

I knew a couple dedicated to service in church but were childless after several years of marriage. By my assessment of them, they seemed happy, and I remember that I was happy when I heard the Lord promise to give them children and even more joy which I believe spurred them to even more service. But I was shocked to find out that somebody was responsible for their childlessness and that that person was a member of the church, one with whom they had closely interacted but who was secretly causing them harm. In church on Sundays, the person would often sit close to them to monitor and evaluate the extent of damage and misery they were experiencing and perhaps draw some satisfaction.

But one day, the Lord spoke through prophecy about all that was going on and what He would do, and that was it; the revelation of what was going on was made, and redemption was granted. After all that, it became clear that the plan of God could no longer be interrupted, and within the preceding year, the couple had a baby.

So, amid all the wickedness, disappointments and failures that you may come across while waiting for the manifestation of God's promises in your life, it is pertinent that you, like the couple in the story just told, and as one of God's real children, develop and put up the kind of attitude that consists of what we will be discussing in the paragraphs below.

Now this attitude we have been pointing to in this chapter refers to the kind that ensures the manifestation of all of God's promises in the life of an individual and should form part of your guide or strategy to get prophecies and all the promises of God manifested in your life just as it did to the house of Israel. To fully grasp what each of the six required actions entails, we shall expand them to better understand what they are about.

Believe the revealed truth

Let us start with this question, are you a believer? I am talking here about being a believer in the promises of God. Do you believe them?

Do you also believe Jesus is the way, truth, life and resurrection? All these questions remain as apposite to the manifestation of prophecy as they have ever been. The reason is that when we believe the Word of God, we also position ourselves to experience His glory. That is why it all starts with believing.

Doubt is the direct opposite of belief and hinders us from experiencing the glory of God. It is more than being spiritual, worthy or prepared but believing whatever God says (John 11:40). The pertinence of dealing with our doubts increases when we have a greater desire to please God through faith. If we allow our faith grow, we become better able to accept and act on the promises of God concerning our lives. Whether these promises are those written in the Bible, felt in our hearts, seen in a dream or spoken by a true prophet, we should accept them in faith because they contain the mind of God about our current situation and form His divine and perfect plan.

Furthermore, when we fill our hearts with faith, we become better poised to receive whatever we desire (Romans 4:20-21). So, when we are ministered to in prophecy, we ought to test what we hear using the word of God to see if we can tie them to each other and while at it, it is a good idea to remember that God, working through His Spirit, cannot promote any form of confusion in the church and will always ensure harmony between His written word and the messages delivered by His prophets. You see, He even respects the rules we adopt in our worship in church services and operates within them. (1 Corinthians 14:33 GNT). This respect ensures that whatever word He sends to the church does not contravene doctrine or the regulations He had hitherto permitted.

Also, consider whatever solution comes with the word that God sends (because every true prophecy reveals a problem and gives a solution that ensures victory), then without wasting time, act on it in total obedience. This kind of response requires a lot of sensitivity. Small wonder Jesus talked about how His sheep hear His voice. They do this because they know it and can differentiate it from those of others trying to get their attention.

A young, educated, and beautiful lady, who was at the time trusting the Lord for a marriage partner, had just gotten engaged to a gentleman when she was invited to a prophetic service by a friend. When she got to the church, she observed how young and flamboyant-looking the Resident Pastor (host) was, who she noticed kept looking around while exchanging comments with another young man, soon to be introduced, as his friend and *the prophet*.

As the service progressed, since wolves do not spare sheep (as earlier stated), the prophet quickly located this young lady and started ministering to her. He began by asking her questions about what she did for a living and her marital status, and then He told her that he had received a message from God to show her who her heaven-ordained husband was. As he spoke, her heartbeat increased because she thought it was her chance to know if she was on the right track. Perhaps God would confirm if the young man whose proposal she had just accepted was the right one. But it did not turn out so. Instead, the prophet told her their host was the person God had chosen for her. The pastor! A married man!! He certainly cannot be the choice of our holy and sovereign God.

So we must carefully consider what we hear to confirm if the Lord has really spoken, even if we have to approach those we are sure of and who have the spirit of God. Up to today, I know of several people that go to their pastors with all sorts of revelations for interpretation or prayer. However, once from the depths of our hearts, we believe that God has spoken, timely obedience should be our next move. That is why accepting the Word of God is so pertinent. Christ Jesus considers it foolishness if we do the opposite (Luke 24:25).

Put up the right attitude

When I was in primary school, the school authorities usually announced a deadline for school fees, after which defaulters were sent out of their classes and back home. On one such occasion, when I was in primary three, my name was on the list of school fee defaulters. So, I received a letter to take back home to my parents a day before the school planned to take action, and that was to be a reminder to my parents advising them to either pay my school fees or keep me at home the following day.

When I got home that afternoon after school, I rushed to my father's room and kept the letter given to me on his bedside cabinet- a place where he wouldn't miss it, in case I fell asleep before he returned. The following morning I dressed for school and waited by the car for him with a gloomy face. As he approached me, he said, "I saw the letter you kept on top of the cabinet. When you get to school, tell your teacher that I will pay your fees today. Tell her to let you stay in class, okay?" And that was it.

When I eventually got to school, everyone was allowed into their classes at first, but after about three hours, teachers started checking for proof of the payment of school fees and sending defaulters out of their classes. In my class, my teacher made a list with my name included, which she read out loud. When I heard my name, I stood up, walked to my teacher and told her exactly what my father had said that morning. She looked at me and asked aloud how she was sure my father would pay while my classmates giggled. Somehow, I found the boldness to respond, and with my eyes teary too. I said: "My daddy doesn't lie. I am telling you the truth. He told me this morning that he would pay today".

I had hardly finished speaking when I heard my classmates rise to greet a tall and smartly dressed army officer who had just walked in.

"Good moooorning sir!" They all sang out in harmony as he walked briskly towards our teacher. Guess who it was? My daddy! And he brought a bank teller to prove he had paid my fees just as he said he would. He looked at me and patted my head gently as he handed the teller he was holding over to my teacher. Then filled with relief and pride, I grabbed his hand and smiled as I heard my teacher humbly say: "Sir, your son was just telling me that you were going to pay his fees today".

The truth is that I can't say what exactly I was thinking that day, and I certainly did not consider if my father would fail in his promise, but all I was determined to do was let my teacher know what he said he would do.

This story, which tells of a little boy's attitude towards a problem, shares a similitude with the kind of attitude we should have when spoken to by our heavenly father. Such a child-like attitude of belief and trust to boldly act on the Word of God is what we should learn from the story. It is the reason why I have shared it with you.

Children usually trust their parents, so whenever they make any request, they don't bother about its affordability or share any other fear their parents may have. The idea here is that if we believe that our God is sovereign and trustworthy, we should take the time to consider His words when He speaks and as children, act on them. This same idea was what Apostle Paul tried to advise the Thessalonians about in his letter to them (1 Thessalonians 5:20).

Do not be double-minded

Those who are double-minded are always indecisive. They hardly get things done. Such people tend to think this way today and that way tomorrow.

They keep changing their minds and cannot be made responsible for bold decisions or to act in response to a message from God in a timely fashion because they always find it difficult to make up their minds at every stage in life. This is serious!

Prophecy communicates God's mind and instruction concerning our current situation to give us victory. It requires quick responses but double-minded people, because of the challenges they have with decision-making, do not always act when they ought to, to manifest the promises of God or even to receive anything from Him (James 1:6-8).

Act on your prophecy

If you believe, act immediately. Be obedient, do what the Lord wants you to do and do it accurately, quickly, happily and expectantly. If God says He wants you to repent, you must understand that it is because He loves you, so you should strive for it genuinely.

Set aside any doubts, worries and anxieties that you may have about the prophecies you receive and submit fully to the Lord. The Bible says we should trust God with all our hearts, and I recommend we do so, just like a little child who trusts his father (Proverbs 3:5-6). Every action we take after receiving a prophecy must show this trust for the one who has spoken and our belief that we know that He has the power to do whatever He says.

God is just as dependable as He has ever been. He can and keeps His promises to us just as He did in the past to the children of Jacob in the Bible (1kings 8:56). Therefore, while waiting for the full manifestation of any prophecy, we ought to ensure that we engage in three highly recommended actions:

1. Pray always

We should pray continuously about all prophecies. It is worth doing because God likes reminders, so even while praying, please remind Him about His promises in those prophecies and whatever He told us while we plead our cases and pour out our hearts. Remember, whatever God says is part of a divine and perfect plan made by Him and to be executed at a time of His choosing (Isaiah 43:26).

Anna, in the Bible was very passionate about the spoken prophecies regarding the redemption of Jerusalem. Even though she was advanced, at age 84, she prayed and fasted passionately concerning all that was to happen. So, when she saw what she had been praying for had started happening, she began to thank God concerning His faithfulness regarding the answers to prayer she witnessed (Luke 2:36-38).

2. Have faith

As Christians, all that we do should be by our faith which comes from the word of God. Without this faith, our everyday actions would be unpleasing to God. For all receivers of prophecy, manifestation comes through faith, and as children of Abraham, we must conduct ourselves like we have hope and the assurance that with God, all things are possible. If we really believe and act like God can do all things, then He will be pleased to fulfil all His promises to us like He did to the house of Jacob.

The proof that we believe is in our action. Our faith is visible in our actions, without which it is not worth much. These actions are informed by hope and the assurance of who we are in Christ and what He can do. This principle works in all circumstances, so act like you have gotten what you wanted despite whatever you see. Act on what God says and not what you see, hear or experience (2 Corinthians 5:7).

3. Start preparing

Preparation is necessary because it shows that you expect something to happen. So if you believe the words of a prophecy that promises you a baby, the proof is in your going out to search for or even buy some baby supplies. It also requires that you re-arrange your house by making it more baby-friendly or even setting up a nursery. If you do such things, what you are expecting becomes more tangible. It shows that you are really expecting a baby promised by God.

Also, if God promises you a promotion at work or a foreign course to enhance your career, your faith would require that you start preparing. Go and get the things you need for the trip, probably clothes for the weather of the place you hope to travel to, and most importantly, start processing your passport. By all means, do not sit and do nothing if you catch my drift.

One of the staff of a prominent organisation had been trusting the Lord to attend a foreign course. She had previously been denied the opportunity for a few years by outgone management without knowing why or do anything, but cry to the Lord. One day, after a new management team, led by someone who refused to let things continue the way they had been, was appointed. The boss heard about the injustice done to staff while reviewing the names on a list for that year's course. He immediately cancelled the list and requested a new one, forcing her name and others, previously omitted, to be added for his approval.

So a corrected list was prepared and approved by the boss. Despite the intervention of her boss, the lady still did not attend the course that year. Guess why? She did not have a passport and could not make one fast enough. This story underscores the need for preparation propelled by faith. In her case, and for someone trusting the Lord for an overseas course, the least she should have done was start preparing. She should have gotten a passport.

4. Keep a record of your prophecy

When you are ministered to through prophecy, write everything down for future reference. Apart from helping you decipher a fake prophet from a true one and help you accurately follow any instruction given in the prophecy for your victory, it will become a record of God's promises for you and others- a document that you can refer to whenever you want to remind God of what He promised you.

Every prophecy is for an appointed time. Have you ever thought about the Lord's response to Habakkuk's complaint, telling him to write down the revelation received to make it plain while awaiting the set time for its manifestation (Habakkuk 2:2-3)? We should always do the same thing today, and while we are at it, ensure that we embrace the following two virtues:

The virtue of patience: If you ever notice strong faith, it must be because its carrier has learned to be patient. Having patience enables us wait for God's appointed time without giving up, even as we prepare ourselves for what God has spoken. There are times when it would seem as though doubt has taken over, with all sorts of suggestions like the one from Sarah to Abraham that led to the birth of Ishmael (Genesis 17:17)

The story ends with Abraham, our father, who is a faith model to us, waiting patiently and eventually getting what God promised him. Like him, we should trust God and allow Him do whatever He promises when He chooses, while we wait patiently (Hebrews 6:15).

Righteousness: Righteousness is a defence. Without holiness, it is impossible to approach the almighty and holy God. While waiting for the manifestation of a prophecy, endeavour to live a life of righteousness and holiness. It requires being consecrated and separated from the world and its attractions (2Corinthians 6:7).

This kind of living carries a lot of power. It is the kind that removes the possibility of getting bumped and bruised by any enemy working against the manifestation of the divine plan of God for your life. It reduces the likelihood of suffering, delay and despair while waiting for the promises of God to manifest. It shall always be well with the righteous (Isaiah 3:10).

5. Discern and honour grace

When we receive Christ as our Lord and Saviour, the Holy Spirit fills us sand gives us a gift that enables us to discern spirits. We are to use this gift in several ways, like identifying a wolf among sheep and perceiving the grace of God upon His servants. In the latter, we must check to see if our spirits agree with what the person says and does. This should be followed by additionally matching their words and actions with the Word of God to lead us to conclude that they are genuine. (1 John 4:1).

Discerning of spirit must never be confrontational. God is the ultimate judge and punisher. The ability to discern protects us as children of God and keeps us from offering ourselves to a wolf disguised as a sheep, only to be led astray. The benefit of our ability to discern is the ability to make the decision of whether to stay among such wolves or speedily leave.

In addition, like the Shunammite woman, the ability to identify grace and take advantage of it attracts breakthroughs. She convinced her husband to allow the provision of meals for Elisha, the prophet, whenever he was in town and eventually prepared a room for him to sleep at night. Her kindness caused Elisha to prophesy concerning her deepest desire to have a child, which gave her a miracle- a son (2 Kings 4:8).

That can be considered a good example of discerning the grace of God on His servant, which we ought not to miss and can take advantage of. It can go beyond identifying and discussing such things to honouring its carrier. Doing so, whether we realise it or not, honours the Lord and ensures that when such servants of God pronounce a blessing, the spirit of God in them (Holy Spirit) responds by bringing such pronouncements to pass. We can provoke God to action and receive a breakthrough when we are good to His genuine servants.

HOW TO RECEIVE A PROPHECY

What this refers to is the proper attitude we should put up when receiving a prophecy. As previously pointed out, we should test all spirit, which includes that of the one prophesying. So whether they pass our test and we feel they are speaking God's truth or otherwise, we are supposed to receive every word of prophecy in humility and prayer.

One reason to be very careful concerning our attitudes when we receive a prophecy is to ensure that we do not grieve the Holy Spirit (Ephesians 4:30). I have heard of people who have reacted in ways that seem inappropriate and which does not communicate the grace that builds others up. They responded in pride or anger because they felt embarrassed or insulted. I have also heard about people who responded in ways that provoked God and got Him to change things in their lives. Some people have responded to prophecy based on a previously strained relationship with the speaker and publicly threaten physical or legal action against them.

That reminds me of a story about a man who was told what was to come and the steps he urgently needed to take by a madman right on the street as he walked home from work. The madman ended his revelation by saying calmly, while looking away from the man's stupefied gaze: "If you do not like what I said, you can sue me."

Suing a madman is quite hilarious, isn't it? The point here is that issues related to prophecy require a lot of sensitivity and patience. We must realise how much God loves us when we are genuinely prophesied to, which is why He sends us these messages. So, when we receive a prophecy, our response should be to the love behind it. That is the most appropriate response.

Receive your prophecy prayerfully

When a prophet is speaking, it is advisable to be in the mood of prayer. While others are being ministered to, we can sing songs of praise, but by all means, we should connect through prayer.

Furthermore, as we receive our prophecy and long afterwards, we should pray and commit whatever we hear into the Lord's hands. Whether we believe and feel good about what was said, its speaker, or totally doubt it, we still need to pray to line up whatever we hear with the word of God and his promises to us.

Receive your prophecy with humility

Ezra Taft Benson[8], an American government official and religious leader who served as the 15th United States Secretary of Agriculture, is known for saying:

"Pride is concerned with who is right; humility is concerned with what is right". (E.T. Benson)

It is not possible to be humble and disrespectful at the same time. Humility involves lowering ourselves in front of others. And in the end, God exalts us.

We should not show pride, conceit or arrogance while receiving a prophecy; it can cause us to grieve the Holy Spirit. I will share a story that conveys this point.

A Senior Deaconess in my church once told us about a prayerful and God-fearing lady she once knew who got married to a man whose family was suffering from a curse. This curse came from fetish practices done by previous generations in the family. They had sacrificed a son, which grieved the community and led to the pronouncement of the curse on them.

It then followed that no member of the family had a son. The curse ensured that they did not. Sons in that part of the country where the lady's husband was from, were culturally desirable and at that time, necessary for passing down a name and inheritance from one generation to the next. Of course, she did not know about all this before marrying her husband and later bore him six daughters. But I want to believe God wanted to change things for her in her marriage and here is why.

One day before a large congregation, she received a strange prophecy accusing her of being evil and responsible for the problems in her immediate and extended family. While this was going on, she knelt in humility and prayed.

Her response seemed to have touched God's heart, and in another service, He spoke to her and said that since she had acted in a way that pleased him by deciding to be humble and not talk back in an attempt to defend herself or embarrass the speaker, He had decided to exalt her by breaking the curse in her family and give her sons. After God spoke, she went on to have six sons.

God visited this lady because of how she received a prophecy. She humbled herself despite the possibly hurtful, shameful and untrue message she received and did not try to dishonour the owner of the church who promises to honour us if we honour Him

(1Samuel 2:30). When we complain, murmur against, physically or verbally abuse or generally dishonour His servant, it is Him that is being dishonoured, not them (Exodus 1:8).

HOW TO REVERSE A NEGATIVE PROPHECY

In the early pages of this book, we examined the reasons for the failure of prophecies. They were similar in many ways to the causes of negative prophecies, and we can work with them to establish a guide to reverse them. Many people are terrified of the manifestation of negative prophecies. They fear the judgment it carries, a response capable of leading them to act in ways that worsen the situation.

Some people say that negative prophecies are irreversible if pronounced by a real man of God but easy to reverse if pronounced by a false one - usually referred to as mere hirelings. Nevertheless, whether they come in the form of judgments, curses or pronouncements, they are kept in existence by remaining in sin, disobedience or wickedness.

Whatever situation attracts a negative prophecy must be dealt with first if there is to be a reversal. We must never despise or disdain God like the children of Eli (Hophni and

Phinehas). The Lord had promised that Eli's family would continue to hold the exalted position of Priests to minister before Him. But due to the wickedness of his sons, this was no longer to be. Instead, there was a negative prophecy against the family. Though addressing negative prophecies is an urgent and necessary decision, it must be thoroughly, sincerely and quickly done to ensure that the underlying causes of such pronouncements are taken care of. To those who experience negative prophecies, rather than display acts of helplessness or dismay, they should carefully address the problem from its roots. If they follow three steps of genuine repentance, crying out to the Lord and locating a higher anointing, they will deal with any negative prophecy and curse.

Genuinely repent

Sins like disobedience are one of the sources of negative prophecies. But such negative prophecies can be swung around by the opportunity available in genuine repentance and commitment to a life of obedience to God. A case in mind is when God sent a message concerning the future to one of the kings of Judah known as Hezekiah (2 Kings 20:16-19). The destruction and captivity that were prophesied, could have all been averted if the four kings that eventually reigned after his great-grandson (King Josiah) had repented and turned from evil. God would have withdrawn

His hand against them, and the fall of Jerusalem avoided.

Also, since negative prophecies come because of sins like disobedience and lies, our starting point in reversing them should be quick repentance and to forsake every sin. It puts an end to the anger of God and attracts His mercy such that it prevails instead of His judgment.

We should avoid giving our lives to Christ when Alter Calls are made at church services, only to take them back after these services but strive to keep our salvation. That reminds me of the day one of my colleagues at work invited me to a service in her church. It was one of the biggest congregations I had ever seen, and service that day was exceptional.

Everything was done differently. As soon as the service ended and we began to leave, I became aware of how illusive the time we had just spent in the church was, with all the smiles, courtesies and orderliness I had just witnessed. As I walked to my car, I observed that as people left, they displayed a noticeable impatience and a bit of arrogance. Many sped past me in reckless showoffs and even competition as I cautiously drove towards the main road through a narrow but smooth road that led out of the church premises.

When I approached the end of the drive, I noticed that too many cars tried to pass simultaneously, which led to a jam, and we all became stuck in one place. Then I heard a man who drove a taxi shout to a sister who had just cut him off:

"Why are you behaving like this? And you are just coming out of the church!"

And she replied in a harsh tone:

"Oga! Abeg leave church out of this"

I am sure she meant that the man should not expect her to conduct herself in Christian Character outside the church. She was wrong.

As for those who see going to church as similar to going to the clinic, that must change. The clinic? You ask, yes! I heard a story about a pastor who ran into a sister he had not seen in church for a while and made the customary comment: "I haven't seen you in service for a while".

Her response shocked him and caused him to remember the first day he had seen her. She had been ill for some time before her first day in his church and looked unhappy and frail when she came. When he made an Alter Call to invite the sick for prayers, she came out and received healing.

He had even prayed for her again after that day when he heard of her financial and family challenges. And this day, while standing before her, he recalled all these and also thought about her character and how regular and punctual she used to be, which had caused him to thank God several times for the many miracles she had received.

But now, as they spoke to each other, the response he had just received in response to his enquiry of not seeing her in church was really unexpected. She told him she would not want to lie to him, but she, honestly, would not be attending church anymore. Then she explained further by asking him in Pidgin English: "If person wen no well go hospital, when hin well, e no go return house?"

This meant that since she had become challenge-free, she had decided to return to her old life. We must strive to remain in Christ Jesus, the source of life. When we find salvation, we must yield to the Spirit of God and be determined not to return to our previous ungodliness (Titus 2:11-14). We must also focus on the cross and the hope that lies ahead that one day, we will see our blessed Saviour.

When we accept Jesus as our Lord and Saviour and taste His goodness, there must be no looking back. So let us continue in faith, marching on like soldiers with no distraction but focused on pleasing our Commanding Officer (2 Timothy 2:4).

Cry out to the Lord in prayer

After repenting of sin, cry out to the Lord and make a case as King Hezekiah did. He listens. In case you do not know this story, it goes that the prophet Isaiah prophesied the death of King Hezekiah. In this prophecy, the king was to put his house in order because he would die. That meant attending to issues concerning his estate and probably naming a successor to the throne, in addition to other things. But on hearing the message of the prophet, the king faced the wall, backed the world and cried out to the Lord from the depths of his heart. He reminded God of how he had obeyed and served Him over the years.

Come on! All that commitment ought to count for something, shouldn't it? Well, I guess it should because God heard his prayer and sent the same prophet back to prophesy a positive message. In this new prophecy, he received additional fifteen years to live and rule as king (Isaiah 38:1-6)

So, concerning any negative prophecy, we must quickly remind God of what He said concerning our lives as His children. God has spoken concerning all sorts of challenges: poverty, death, failure etc. All we just need to do is remind Him - firstly about His word concerning these things and secondly about our love, dedication, service etc. That's why we should live in a way that earns God's approval.

It requires working for God in purposeful service and showing love for Him and men so that He can look at us and our service and use it (as a reason) to show us mercy.
Remember the price our Lord paid on the cross, giving His life to free us from our sins and the problems and curses they attract.

We should allow the blood shed on the cross to complete its work and give us enduring victory over every foe and the darkness they operate through. There is mighty power in the blood of Jesus available to as many as will look to the finished work on the cross.

Locate a higher anointing

Whenever there are negative declarations, pronouncements or curses made by a prophet or someone of spiritual authority, our response should, in addition to genuine repentance for the offence committed, include praying to the Lord for direction to someone of higher anointing than the one who made the pronouncement who would not only guide us on our journey to freedom but also pray by the power and authority of the Holy Spirit to cancel any negative declaration or pronouncement.

In the Bible, when Jacob spoke and made negative pronouncements about Reuben (Genesis 49:2-4), these pronouncements came to pass and remained for about five hundred years until Moses reversed them before his death (Deuteronomy 33:6). Joshua also cursed the city of Jericho after the battle that led to its destruction in Joshua 6:26. This curse led to the contamination of the waters of Jericho, and it remained so until Elisha broke it. The Bible records in 2Kings2:18-22 how Elisha purified the waters and land in Jericho.

Anointing truly breaks the yoke, so the pronouncement of a higher spiritual authority nullifies a previously existing one and the situation it caused. When carriers of this anointing speak by the mercy and will of God, the power of God is released to turn things around.

Generally, every negative prophecy is sure to turn around when we run to the Lord and begin a relationship with Him. Salvation is free today because Jesus paid the ultimate price. As hearers of the gospel, one of the great choices we can make in life is to accept this salvation and the hand of fellowship that the Lord offers.

To choose a relationship with Christ Jesus has been a life-changer for many people. But some of them wonder why many of the prophecies concerning their lives fail. The over three thousand promises made through Bible revelations do not target just anybody but the real children of God, leaving us with a choice of faith.

So far, we can see that a better understanding of prophecy offers an opportunity to take advantage of its purpose and power. It also guides us to God's love. As a result, it seems like a good idea to carry on every effort needed to manifest prophecy by developing the qualities and attitudes espoused in the pages of this book which are still necessary even today, to make all prophecy come to pass.

---

[8] http://en.wikipedia.org/wiki/Ezra_Taft_Benson

BOOKS BY THE AUTHOR

I am glory: Breaking through obscurity

There is a way to attract all you will ever need in this life. It is one that makes you one of those so loved by God, that they draw His attention and loyalty. Pastor and teacher U.K. Tommy can help you find it.

I am Glory: Breaking through obscurity is a bold declaration of self. It is a presentation of a person we could become if we are obedient enough, knowledgeable enough, bold enough, strong enough, and determined enough. It offers the assurance that God still clothes His real children with glory even now when there are so many reasons to accept mediocrity and the deception as the standard.

In this memoir is a powerful guide to help you take on the challenge of breaking through your obscurity so that you can begin to:

- Get answers to all your prayers

- Stop pursuing things but attract them into your life

- Become prosperous in all you do

- Live beyond spiritual errors and reap the full benefits of your kingdom service

www.ingramcontent.com/pod-product-compliance
Lightning Source LLC
Chambersburg PA
CBHW031459160726
47994CB00005B/2112